T5-BQA-317

Schössler · Weede

West German Elite Views on National Security and Foreign Policy Issues

Sozialwissenschaftliches Forum
Band 1

Herausgegeben von
Paul Kevenhörster und Franz Lehner

Dietmar Schössler · Erich Weede

West German Elite Views on National Security and Foreign Policy Issues

Foreword by Morton A. Kaplan

Athenäum Verlag Königstein/Ts.
1978

CIP-Kurztitelaufnahme der Deutschen Bibliothek

Schössler, Dietmar:
West German elite views on national security and foreign policy issues / Dietmar Schössler, Erich Weede. Foreword by Morton A. Kaplan. – Königstein/Ts.: Athenäum Verlag, 1978.
(Sozialwissenschaftliches Forum, Bd. 1)
ISBN 3–7610–8207–X

NE: Weede, Erich:

Umschlaggestaltung: Gerhard Keim, Frankfurt/M.
Gesamtherstellung: Friedrich Pustet, Regensburg
Printed in Germany
ISBN 3-7610-8207-X

Foreword

Germany is both a divided state and the keystone of the western defense against the Soviet Union and its allies. The opinions of élite groups in West Germany, therefore, will play a significant role with respect to deterrence, détente, and the transformation of the world political system. By élite, Schössler and Weede are referring to the middle level élite groups. They made no effort to survey the leaders of the political parties or the top officers among the services.

Drs. Schössler and Weede warn us there is no way of defining élites such that we can employ a representative sample. Yet their sample is sufficiently broad with respect to the SPD, the CDU and the CSU, age groups, and military and civilians to provide reasonable reassurance that their evidence is genuinely representative. They have surveyed 864 élite respondents on the basis of some 200 items and background variables. This impressive sample is bolstered by the penetrating and distinguishing questions that the respondents were asked.

On the basis of the responses, Schössler and Weede believe that the respondents fall into categories that may be labelled realism and idealism, although they agree that these are very loose terms and do not wish to imply the lack of realism of those who are categorized as idealistic. By realism they mean people who, by and large, place faith in strength or deterrence while the idealists are those who place much greater faith in détente. The idealists believe that economic cooperation between East and West promotes peace, that the CSCE has been a success and should be institutionalized, and that the attitude of the West toward MBFR should be conciliatory. Idealists tend to believe that unilateral concessions may help to overcome the arms race, which they view as a major factor leading to the outbreak of war.

However, on the whole, the majority in every classification, including occupation, age, and education – 70.3% of the overall sample – subscribes to deterrence as the best method of coping with the Soviet bloc. Only 17.1% of the sample identify conflicts of security interest that are produced by arms races as a cause of war. 82.9% reject the notion that the tension caused by an arms buildup produces wars.

Furthermore, only 8.7% of the respondents say that the threat from the Warsaw Treaty Organization powers has decreased and 55.2% perceive an increased threat. Undoubtedly related to this is the belief of 62.9% of the sample that „the small and middle-sized European nations contribute to security in Europe, if they accept the leadership of their respective superpower."

Actually, a majority of respondents support CSCE; but the majority is only barely such among those who subscribe to deterrence. On the other hand, majority opinion favors a hard line on MBFR. 68.4% of the respondents do not see any favorable impact of economic cooperation and détente upon military risk.

However, another significant factor quickly emerges. The belief in deterrence is a belief in a second-best system. This is shown by the fact that 41.8% of the respondents believe that deterrence „merely decreases the risk of war." This may be the reason why a solid majority of the respondents favor a more active foreign policy for the Federal Republic. Of those who argue for activism, 85% are thinking of activism in the political sphere while only 24% favor a more active defense policy.

The respondents strongly favor cross-Atlantic ties and European ties for Germany. Furthermore, with respect to Europe, 56% favor full economic integration; 36% favor social and welfare policy integration; and 81.8%favor foreign and defense policy integration. Overall a solid 74% of the respondents favor extremely close defense ties between Germany and her western European neighbors as well as with the United States. Very few of the respondents favor an independent German military posture.

The élites responded in very interesting ways to the Soviet bloc. There is roughly an equal split among those who favor increases, stagnation, or decreases in Comecon internal political integration. On the issue of Comecon internal economic integration, only 25% of the sample favored a decrease. 43.2% of the sample favored a decrease in Warsaw Treaty Organization military integration and a surprisingly high 18% desired greater WTO military integration.

The responses of the military élite were quite interesting. There was consistent opposition to a nationalistic policy while corollary work by other social scientists in Germany indicates a decrease of authoritarian attitudes during military service. Union members and foreign policy researchers favored deterrence, but by relatively narrow margins. The median position for union members and foreign policy researchers on the defense budget was that of constancy, although fewer favored decreases than favored increases. No category in the survey favored a decrease in the defense budget although those who favored a constant defense budget outnumbered those who favored an increase by a margin of 2 to 1. Rather large majorities (in the neighborhood of 7 to 1) among union members and foreign policy researchers believe that détente avoids war, although the majority even here rejects the notion that arms races produce war by 3 to 1 and 2 to 1 margins, respectively. However, the majority against the "arms-races-produce-war" syndrome is far higher among those who do not fall into those two categories.

There is one very important point on which the élites and masses seem to differ. On the basis of independent studies, only 51% of the mass public prefers a U.S. military connection while 38% prefers a Swiss-type neutrality. The élite position as we have mentioned is far stronger on these issues. Thus, despite all the differences among the élites, we are not surprised to learn that the élites are strong supporters of NATO, the European common market, and political negotiations with the Soviet Union and its allies.

Although the masses of the German public are not as firmly convinced of the former positions as are the élites, the preponderance of élite opinion demonstrates the depth of the support within Germany for the current system of world politics. However, one must always keep in mind that these opinions are expressed within the framework of belief and circumstance that sustains them. A strong shock to the entire system, some completely unexpected development, or some massive failure by the United States or West Germany's western allies might disrupt the entire constellation of belief and force it within a new frame. What the survey does indicate is the potential stability of this body of opinion provided that policies are followed by all the major nations that avoid the types of shocks that could produce revolutionary change in opinion. Nothing in public-opinion studies themselves can guarantee the intelligence of national leaderships, the absence of revolutionary upheavals elsewhere, or the kindness of fate.

This excellent study provides us with important information concerning the state of public opinion as a resource for intelligent policies by the leaderships of the democratic states. The proper utilization of that tool is the responsibility of the top leaderships.

Morton A. Kaplan

Table of Contents

Preface

The data analyzed in this paper derive from Schössler's SIPLA project. Its rationale is outlined in Enke, Schmidt, Schössler (1976). Previously, Enke and Schössler (1977) published a short report on those findings which concern CSCE. The SIPLA project has been funded by the German Society for Peace and Conflict Research („Deutsche Gesellschaft für Friedens- und Konfliktforschung, DGFK"). We gratefully acknowledge DGFK's assistance. Erika Brückner and Ursula Hoffmann-Lange, both from ZUMA-Mannheim, helped to improve the questionnaire. Moreover, Edo Enke (Gesamthochschule Wuppertal) and Peter Schmidt (Universität Mannheim) have been deeply involved at various stages of the SIPLA project. We are grateful for all the help and advice we received from these people. The responsibility for arguments and conclusions, however, rests solely with the authors. This book is merely a partial report of some SIPLA results. It concerns those domains where Schössler's interest in national security planning or policy implementation overlap Weede's interest in power politics and related theories.

Why do we publish this report in English rather than in German? Firstly, English is the lingua franca of contemporary social science. Secondly, our respondents are quite cosmopolitan in their sources of information and quite supportive of European-American cooperation. A book written in English is simultaneously accessible to most of our respondents and to our American and other European friends. Finally, information-sharing with foreign friends and colleagues fits an open society as well as the purposes of science.

Introduction

The major purpose of this study is to describe elite views on national security and foreign policy. Such a descriptive exercise derives meaning when elite views are embedded within some explanatory framework; when assumptions about determinants and consequences of elite views are introduced. While we make such assumptions in the interpretation of our findings, we want to clarify, at the very outset, that we do not test most of these assumptions within this work.

Regarding consequences of elite views first, we expect them to have some impact on decision-making. Social-psychological research, of course, warns us against too facile inferential leaps from attitudes to behavior; from saying to doing. While we are aware of these problems, we do not pursue them. We admit that our interpretations of elite views rest on nothing better than common sense — as do almost all available interpretations of elite views on national security and foreign policy. Nevertheless, we believe that common-sense reasoning based on a more adequate description of elite views is preferable to common sense based on a less adequate description thereof.

Regarding background conditions or possible determinants of elite views, we investigate the differences among various social groups. Do people who belong to different political parties provide different answers to national security items? Do military experience, status, or rank make a difference? Are there any differences between trade union members, foreign policy or peace researchers, and other elite members? Do old and young respondents think alike or differently? All these questions refer to variation within the West German elite. Therefore, these questions may be investigated with our data. However, there is another set of determinants of elite views which we deem to be of great importance. In our opinion, elite views somehow respond to the position a nation occupies in world politics; to involvement in conflicts of interest and geostrategic factors. Take a simple example: Perceptions of threat are likely to be related to capabilities of other nations as well as to presence or absence of friendly ties to powerful nations. While domestic social groups may influence variation within national elites, positions in world politics and geostrategic factors are likely to influence the mean or central tendency of national elite opinion. Obviously, data on one national elite do not permit testing of the latter type of proposition. However, there is at least some weak cross-national evidence available (discussed below) to support our views on the impact of position and geostrategic factors. Moreover, we feel that it is perfectly legitimate to interpret our data within some explanatory framework that is not tested here, albeit testable in principle.

While we do not restrict our interest in elite views to causal assertions, there are definitely some items included that refer to such assertions. We want to find out what implicit or explicit theories/propositions about world politics our respondents believe in. Nevertheless, we do not engage in cognitive mapping, as has been done by Axelrod (1976). Firstly, if you do not restrict yourself to causal assertions, cognitive mapping becomes something between extremely difficult and impossible. Secondly, our focus of interest differs from how people draw conclusions from complex belief systems and from related questions.

While Schössler's and Weede's interests sufficiently overlap to make cooperation possible and meaningful, our interests are not identical. As our data come from Schössler's SIPLA project (see Enke, Schmidt, Schössler 1976 for a brief outline), we portray Schössler's interests implicitly by reference to the larger project. The SIPLA project intends to achieve something different from conventional survey research. That is why at least some participants in our survey took a much more active role than survey respondents ordinarily do. In a series of workshops, Schössler tried to investigate which questions elites and potential participants find most interesting. Actually, some questions have been proposed, discussed, and formulated at these workshops by participants rather than being imposed by researchers. Based on Schössler's notion of a segmented strategy community in the FRG, these workshops had the double function of stimulating discussion between members of different segments and of preparing a meaningful discourse on national security issues within the SIPLA context. After assuring that the questionnaire would be perceived as meaningful and relevant by potential participants from quite diverse backgrounds, the questionnaire was distributed — mainly via official channels in hierarchical organizations like political parties, trade unions, armed forces or the department of defense; from the top downwards. We are well aware of the fact, of course, that such a procedure implies some loss of control on the researcher's part about "sampling" procedures.

While survey research in general tries not to affect, but merely to assess opinions, the SIPLA project is to do both. In a first step, SIPLA collects elite opinions. Our present text emphasizes a description and discussion thereof. Nevertheless, the reader should get a feeling for the broader perspective of SIPLA, because participants are well aware of that. In a second step, SIPLA results from the first questionnaire have been fed back to our participants. The promise to trade filling out a single questionnaire against opinion data from the total sample, has been a major incentive to ensure collaboration from participants. In a third step, i.e. after being informed about elite opinion in general and after knowing where one stands relative to elite opinion in general or relative to one's own subgroup, participants have received a second questionnaire. Again, the major purpose thereof is not to conduct an ordinary panel survey in order to evaluate trends in opinion. Instead, SIPLA is to study how the feedback of information to respondents affects opinions of their own, to see where which groups change opinions after being exposed to other views, and to elite consensus or within-elite dissent. Such a research strategy is related, of course, to the DELPHI method, or, more exactly, to its policy version (Linstone and Turoff 1975). In particular, we would like to find out where information increases consensus and where information either creates or reinforces polarization. Moreover, if successful, SIPLA is a means for elite segments to take into account each other's views, to discuss them with each other (e.g., at future workshops) and to overcome segmentation.[1]

While Schössler's interests are heavily on the applied side, on working with national security experts and elites, on experimenting with new forms of communication among them, and on improving the quality of national security debates, Weede's interests are somewhat different. Weede is particularly interested in the comparison of causal assertions made by elites and causal assertions which resist falsification, if under scrutiny in quantitative-empirical research on world politics. While some such comparisons have been done already (Weede 1977b, Weede and Schössler 1978), they are excluded from this text. The importance of such comparisons of real world causal relations (provided that one accepts the quantitative-empirical approach as a means to getting at them) and believed-in causal relations is obvious. False beliefs may prepare false decisions. However, communication between quantitative-empirical researchers and decision-making elites should not be considered as a one-way street where researchers tell decision-makers what true causal dependencies look like. Quite to the contrary, for the time being, at least as important, if not more so, is to inform researchers about views held by strategic experts, political elites and decision-makers. After all, these views rather than researchers' views are more likely to affect the course of events. Therefore, causal assertions made by political elites should be placed high on the agenda for quantitative-empirical research. Who gains most, and in what time perspective, from such a communication process between researchers and other elites, is an open question. Researchers might gain quite a bit, if Burns (1968, p. 17) comes even close to the truth: "Most of the moves in world politics look quite crude; yet one recognizes that World Affairs is among the few subjects of study in which the persons investigated are for the most part much more gifted and intelligent than those investigating their behavior". Causal ideas from elites may be a source of alternative theorizing and even help researchers to improve on their own theorizing. In our opinion, any such help is still needed.

The universe of thinkable items on national security and foreign policy is much larger than can be handled in any questionnaire, especially if respondents have as little time as elites do. The lion's share of our items comes from Schössler's discussions, workshops, and pretests with potential participants, as well as with some social science students. Schössler's major concern in selecting items has been an effort to produce a questionnaire that is perceived as meaningful by respondents; one that reflects their interests and concerns. However, some items (e.g. no.27) reflect Weede's (1975, 1976) theorizing, as well as results from his quantitative work.

Elite surveys pose a series of methodological and theoretical problems which national opinion surveys lack. First, what is an elite? Although we use formal positions in bureaucratic organizations, institutions, associations, parties, business and the military as a criterion, we do not believe in elite being a well-defined universe. It is extremely difficult to tell who belongs to an elite. We can easily agree with such statements as made by Deutsch and Edinger (1959, p. 60): "Much of foreign policy is determined by various elites, while the general public is only indirectly involved. Such elites are, generally speaking, those groups in the population who are better informed about policy matters and who have greater influence upon policy decisions than the rest of their countrymen." Of the two criteria of information and of influence, the latter one is obviously crucial. If elites are influential by definition and if influence is a matter of degree, then one might even call into question a dichotomous concept of elite as maintained by Dahrendorf (1961, p. 215), where one is either in or out, and replace it with some continuous concept like "eliteness", of which one may be characterized by more or less.[2] Rather than being a simple dichotomy, belongingness to an elite might come closer to a continuum where all thinkable cutting points are somewhat arbitrary. If there is no clear cutpoint then there is no well-defined universe. Without having a well-defined universe, random or representative sampling is impossible. We do not claim to have anything better than an "accidental sample" and are well aware of the fact that any generalization from such a base is extremely hazardous. Utmost caution in evaluation of our findings is essential. Nevertheless, we believe that an accidental sample of 864 elite respondents, about 200 items, and background variables from a standardized questionnaire is definitely preferable to even less information which each of us may be able to collect via personal contacts and conversations and then interpret according to an implicit rather than a reproducible calculus. We are not aware of any study of elite views on national security that really moves beyond accidental sampling. While we are not prepared to suppress any criticism against accidental sampling, we feel that insistence on anything better leaves us with something even worse: no systematic data gathering and data analysis at all.

Lacking a well-defined universe of elites and a list of addresses of potential participants, Schössler looked for a practical solution. He approached influential, and often leading members of all kinds of organizations that are important either in setting the framework for debate on national security issues, in preparing political decisions at the expert level, in implementing political decisions or that might criticize and oppose any decisions made. The influentials whom Schössler approached in the first half of 1976,[3] themselves took over the data collection within their respective organizations. In addition, some persons have been approached on an individual basis. Finally, Schössler collected 864 questionnaires out of an original 1800 mailed out, i.e., he achieved a response rate slightly below 50 percent. A look at Russett and Hanson (1975 who did only slightly better in a US survey on similar topics,) demonstrates such a response rate is reasonable for an elite survey of our sample size and topic. Of course, access proved to be much more of a problem in some places and organizations than elsewhere. The following table provides a summary of our sample composition as well as the difficulties in obtaining the data.

Our elite sample is somewhat biased in favor of those who actively belong to either the armed forces or supporting associations. The next largest group is formed by party members and party workers. Unions, business, media and education are less well represented in our sample. However, national security is of much

Composition of the SIPLA sample by channel of access

	N	%	response-rate (%)
Christian Democrats (CDU + CSU)	86	10.0	24 - 36
Social Democrats (SPD)	122	14.1	47
Liberal Democrats (FDP)	49	5.7	33
Trade Unions	69	8.0	25 - 63
Industrial Management	65	7.5	66
Mass Media	52	6.0	51
Foreign Policy or Peace Research	57	6.6	49
Armed Forces and Department of Defense	139	16.1	53
Military Associations	200	23.1	52
Other	25	2.9	-
	864	100	

Numbers in the first three rows refer to those who have been accessed via party channels. This number is not identical to party members in our sample.

Most trade union members belong to either the union for public services, transport and traffic (ÖTV), i.e. to a public employees union, or work with the German Federation of Trade Unions (DGB).

Industrial management refers primarily to those in the armaments and related business.

Military associations include reserve soldiers' associations, officers' associations, and a society for military and security affairs.

Two numbers within the last column indicate that response rate greatly differs in various subgroups.

---

higher concern for armed forces and supporting associations, as well as for political parties who either govern or would like to do so, than for other social groupings.

Moreover, our sample is biased in another way. In the West German legislative, Social Democrats (SPD) and Liberals (FDP) combined, only slightly exceed the number of Christian Democrats (CDU + CSU). In our sample, however, there are 226 Social Democrats and 62 Liberals versus a mere 173 Christian Democrats, 62 of whom belong to the Bavarian branch (CSU) of the party. If one uses legislative strength as a standard, then ruling Social Democrats and Liberals are overrepresented at the expense of Christian Democrats; or more exactly at the expense of Christian Democrats outside of Bavaria. Whether one should consider oversampling of ruling parties and undersampling of opposition parties as bias might be disputed. After all, ruling parties more directly influence politics. If one calls our sample biased, as we are somewhat inclined to do, it is biased in favor of the left, as far as party membership is concerned. If the military were more conservative, in its views, than West German elites in general, then the leftist bias due to oversampling of Social Democrats an Liberals might be partially balanced or overbalanced by a conservative bias due to military oversampling.

There is a third kind of bias in our survey. Most of our respondents do not belong to the most powerful elite members. Our sample does not include Chancellor Schmidt, Minister of Defense Apel, Minister of Foreign Affairs Genscher, Opposition Leaders Kohl and Strauß, nor Social Democratic Party Leader Brandt. Probably, we have moved up somewhat higher with the military and industrial management than elsewhere, but in general our respondents belong to the broad group of those elite members who cooperate with "top" elites, prepare decisions for them, provide them with expert advice, oversee and direct implementation of decisions taken by them, and finally, some of whom stand a chance of being coopted into the top elite later. Although such a bias against truly topmost elites is often found in elite surveys (for very practical reasons), one is forced to reconsider the question whether and why such a survey should or might be called an "elite" survey. At some point in time, we considered the idea of calling our elite survey an expert survey instead. This would avoid connotations of direct political power and influence by stressing technical competence instead. Indeed, many of our respondents do possess such technical competence in foreign and national security affairs and should do so according to their formal positions. Others, however, probably do so to a much lesser degree. Moreover, calling our respondents "experts" rather than "elites" might imply the claim that they are right rather than wrong. Although we are sympathetic to the foreign policy outlook of the majority of our respondents, we feel such an implicit endorsement is premature. While it may be difficult to ascertain how much political influence our respondents wield, it is even more difficult to say to what extent they and we are right or wrong.[4] That is why we prefered the term elite over expert, inspite of our exclusion of top elites. However, our respondents are well educated, concerned about national security problems, and quite likely to be influential. The table following records formal educational achievements.

By collapsing three rows from this table, you see that about 40 percent of our respondent successfully completed university, receiving at least the equivalent of a master's degree. This is a much higher percentage than is found in the German populace. If one adds those who qualified to enter university and sometimes spent some years there, one moves beyond 70%

If indeed, we did survey security elites, our respondents should demonstrate much interest and concern for such matters. Therefore, we asked our participants: "To what degree are you concerned about security policy questions? (Inwieweit fühlen Sie sich selbst von sicherheitspolitischen Fragen betroffen?)" More than 56% of our respondents said they are professionally concerned about national security-related matters, whereas 1.3% denied any concern. More than 20% each professed either "concern" without having professional duties in the area, or "concern" as one out of a couple of professional concerns.

	N	%
Ordinary secondary school only (Hauptschule, Volksschule, Mittelschule oder Gymnasium ohne Abschluß)	115	13.4
Equivalent of US high school (Mittlere Reife)	132	15.2
University entrance examination ("Abitur" which is comparable to two or three years of college)	260	31.2
University diploma (Diplom, Staatsexamen; comparable to M.A.)	201	23.2
Ph.D. (Dr.)	125	14.5
Advanced research work (Habilitation)	17	2.0
Non-response	14	1.6
	864	100

Most of our respondents received a much better education than most Germans did. They are more concerned about national security than most Germans are, and they do have much better access to information than do most people. We see that 35.8% claim to receive some inside information about national security matters, 49.2% claim to be informed via party channels, and 21.5% claim to receive information from the International Institute for Strategic Studies in London and its publications. Remarkably, IISS is a much more important source of information among our respondents than German research institutions. The second most important source of information, again, is a foreign institution, i.e. SIPRI in Stockholm. One has to testify some cosmopolitanism to our respondents.

Formal education, professional concern, and access to information may be important characteristics of elites. What finally counts, however, for political elites, is influence on decision-making. As seen, 53.4% belong to one of the major parties which are represented in the German Bundestag. Even more, i.e. 62.3%, claim some political influence via party channels. In addition, some feel to have some influence via trade unions, business, interest groups, or churches. While we see no possibility to verify in any detail these judgements about political influence, it is obvious that our respondents look more like elites rather than like ordinary citizens.

The limitation of this study is fairly obvious, as is the difficulty of doing better.

There are only four even remotely similar studies on German elites. In 1964, Deutsch et al. (1967) made a survey on German elites where attitudes on foreign policy and national security were covered. Deutsch's study differs from ours in a variety of aspects. While he had 173 respondents, we had 864. While he collected similar data for France, we did not. While he used oral or face-to-face interviews and a fairly unstandardized " questionnaire", we had a written survey and a much more standardized procedure. Finally, of course, there are 12 years between his survey and ours. Inspite of all those differences in time, sample, and procedure, we found some highly similar results (reported below).

In 1964, Schatz (1970) undertook another survey covering 80 members of the German Bundestag, 46 of whom have been members of its defense committee. While his questionnaire is similarly standardized, as ours is, it covers a much wider variety of topics. Nevertheless, some of his results come fairly close to ours.

In 1968, Wildenmann (1968,1971) and his associates (e.g. Schleth 1971) made an elite survey with 808 respondents. Finally, in 1972, Kaltefleiter and Wildenmann sponsored another elite survey with 1825 respondents (Hoffmann-Lange 1976). Given different foci of interest and a comparative lack of military representation, comparability is quite low, so far as our central topics are concerned. Nevertheless, these surveys may be used to make some weak tests of our sampling procedures.

Our sample size compares favorably with that from most other surveys of West German elites. While sample size is one factor in generating confidence in survey findings, it is far from being the only one or even most important one. In order to generalize, we should know something about the representativeness of our sample for West German elites in general. For reasons outlined above, a strict and satisfying answer to the question of representativeness is impossible. But we know from earlier research (Deutsch and Edinger 1959, Hoffmann-Lange 1976, Wildenmann 1971, Zapf 1965) that Protestants and those who do not profess any religious affiliation more frequently hold elite positions than do Catholics. While there is an almost equal number of Catholics and Protestants in West Germany; within the elite, Protestants outnumber Catholics ca. 2:1.[5] If our survey would produce a major deviation from that, it might be due to sampling bias. Fortunately, it does not. Admittedly, this is an extremely weak and somewhat far-fetched test of representativeness, but probably better than no test at all.

As seen, 39.7% of our respondents hold some university degree. Other surveys succeeded in sampling better formally-educated elites. Wildenmann (1971, p. 50) reports 58% for his 1968 sample, whereas Hoffmann-Lange (1976, p. 34) reports a staggering 70.2% for her 1972 sample. At least part of that divergence might be due to either comparative oversampling of administrative and bureaucratic elites in other surveys, or to military oversampling in our survey.

To summarize, our sample is biased in favor of national security and military elites. Its formal educational achievements are somewhat less than for other German elite studies, and Social Democrats are oversampled at the expense of Christian Democrats, except for Bavarian Christian Democrats.

German Elite Views: Pattern of Responses

If one is faced with plenty of data, one must somehow reduce the data set. We experimented with a variety of procedures: 1. Factor analysis, which we based on Pearson product-moment correlations as well as on gamma correlations, where we applied Varimax as well as oblique rotations. 2. Multidimensional scaling based on gamma as a measure of similarity. 3. Ordinary as well as hierarchical clustering based on gamma correlations.

Rather than provide a detailed discussion of those techniques and their adequacy to the problem at hand or their comparative advantages, we merely outline why we even tried something different from the most widely used technique, i.e. factor analysis based on product-moment correlations.

First, our items do not constitute interval scales. Scales are but ordinal. Moreover, most scales use a very limited number of categories and many scales are mere dichotomies.[6] Second, most of our items are characterized by heavily skewed distributions.[7] If variables differ in degree and direction of skewness, marginal distributions enforce deflated product-moment correlations, often severely so. Factor analysis based on such deflated correlations is not an ideal technique and its results should not be taken too seriously.[8]

As the variety of techniques employed produced somewhat similar results (we use those results for little more than as an organizing principle in describing our data), we need not bore and burden the reader with further technical detail. We may as well describe results obtained from our factor analysis based on product-moment coefficients which happen to be more similar to other results obtained than those results are among each other.[9]

Because of asymmetric and skewed distributions of scales, correlations among our 52 foreign policy and national security items tend to be quite low. That is why communalities are generally low, why we need many factors to adequately describe our data set, and why the first three and most potent factors merely account for 25% of the total variance. Inspite of an oblique rotation, the first three factors turned out to be nearly orthogonal, i.e., the maximum correlation among factors has been 0.06. The first factor may be called either "Realism — Idealism" or "Deterrence — Détente"; the second one "Proposed Role for the Federal Republic"; and the third one "North Atlantic Community". In general, responses to items loading on the "Realism"-factor do not account for much variance in those items loading on the "Role for the Federal Republic"-factor or on the "North Atlantic Community"-factor.

For the first factor, we chose the labels "Realism-Idealism" or "Deterrence-Détente" inspite of some problems. First, there are different kinds of Realism and of Idealism. Some "Realists" are likely to disagree with the majority of our respondents concerning the importance of ideological controversy as a cause of war. Nevertheless, most items loading high on the "Realism" or "Deterrence" pole of the first factor strongly remind us of the "Realist" school of thought. That is why we chose the label "Realism". Inspite of some sympathy for some " Realist" views on our part, we definitely do not choose the label "Realism" in order to convey the impression that "Realist" views are realistic. Whether they are or are not, is well beyond the scope of this study.

Moreover, there are different approaches to deterrence and détente. Some scientists or politicians might argue that deterrence and détente complement each other (e.g. Rosecrance 1975), or even that détente presupposes deterrence (e.g. Sonnenfeldt 1978). Without passing any judgment on this point, all we do is assert that among our respondents you rarely find people who both firmly support deterrence and hope strongly for détente (compare Schwarz 1972). Whatever one's position on the true or real meaning of Realism and deterrence, and of Idealism and détente, we propose to accept those labels as nominal definitions and memory aids.

"Realism" or support of "Deterrence" is indicated by the following set of beliefs: The strategic situation in Europe is bad and a source of serious concern. It is likely to change for the worse in the 1980s. Deterrence does contribute to peace. Western defense effort is a response to Soviet threat rather than a consequence of domestic interests in high defense spending. The West German defense budget should be increased for the sake of national security. Arms exports to other-than-NATO nations should be promoted. Political and military cooperation between Western Europe and the United States should be as close as possible. Small- and middle-sized European nations should accept a leading role of their respective superpowers for the sake of peace. Ideological controversy is a major cause of war. By and large, this factor pole is related to items which favor a tough approach to national security issues.

The other pole of the first factor has been called "Idealism" or "Détente", because it refers to the following set of views: Economic cooperation between East and West promotes peace. CSCE has been a success and should be institutionalized. The West should adopt a conciliatory rather than a tough attitude concerning MBFR and the "balance" aspect thereof. Unilateral concessions may help to overcome the arms race. An atmosphere of détente does promote peace. Arms races are a major source of war.

The second factor concerns advocacy of a more active role for the Federal Republic, especially in the political sphere, definitely less in the military sphere, and about as much in East-West and North-South relations or in the UN context.

The third factor concerns items which express an expectation or desire for close links between the US and Western Europe and, to a somewhat lesser degree, an expectation and desire for closer sooperation among Western Europeans. Remarkably low is the loading of an item which favors close defense cooperation among Western Europeans. By contrast, the corresponding US — Western Europe military cooperation item has a much higher loading. There are merely two items with substantial loadings on two factors, i.e., desire for American-European cooperation in foreign policy and defense which belong to the "Realism"-or "Deterrence"-factor as well as to the "North Atlantic Community"-factor.

Realism – Idealism or Deterrence – Détente

Having said something about the pattern of correlations in our data, we may move to some particular items as well as to some cross-tabulations. A typical, i.e., high loading item from the "Realist" or "Deterrence" pole of the first factor is the following:

"In your opinion, did the military and strategic concept of deterrence work? (Hat sich Ihrer Meinung nach das militär-strategische Konzept der Abschreckung bewährt?)"

Deterrence promotes peace (Abschreckung ist friedenserhaltend)	17.9%
Deterrence promotes peace better than other measures do (Abschreckung verringert die Kriegsgefahr besser als andere Maßnahmen)	33.7%
Deterrence merely decreases the risk of war (Abschreckung verringert lediglich die Kriegsgefahr)	41.8%
Deterrence neither promotes peace nor war (Abschreckung ist weder friedenserhaltend noch kriegstreibend)	4.3%
Deterrence tends to lead to war (Abschreckung ist eher kriegstreibend)	2.2%

Here as well as in later tables percentages refer to 864 minus number of missing responses. Here, we lose 13 cases due to missing data. We never fall below 740 cases.

As we can see from this item, most of the German elite evaluates deterrence fairly positively. One out of six subscribes to deterrence without any qualification, slightly more than half feel that there is no substitute to deterrence which equals its effectiveness, more than 90 percent admit at least some effectiveness of deterrence, whereas a meager 2.2% definitely object to a policy of deterrence. Or, there is a fairly strong consensus in the German elite on this basic item.

Because of the fundamental importance of deterrence in national security issues, another item referring to deterrence has been included in our questionnaire:

"On what is the present situation of no-war between East and West primarily based? (Worauf beruht Ihrer Meinung nach die gegenwärtige Situation des Nicht-Krieges zwischen Ost und West in erster Linie?")

Respondents were asked to choose one out of four possible explanations:

On mutual economic interests (auf wechselseitigen wirtschaftlichen Interessen)	13.3%
On the system of military deterrence (auf dem militärischen Abschreckungs-system)	70.3%
On common interests of the superpowers against third parties (auf gemeinsamen Interessen der Supermächte gegenüber Dritten)	9.1%
On an athmosphere of détente since the end of the cold war (auf der entspannten Athmosphäre seit dem Ende des Kalten Krieges)	6.5%

Again, a solid two-thirds majority expresses belief in deterrence. By contrast, no item found less approval than the one which counts détente as a major factor for the avoidance of war. It is obviously not a special phrasing, but a firmly rooted and broadly-based belief in deterrence that produces such answers. A simple cross-classification of these two deterrence items may serve as a tool for reliability assessment. Before, the five-options multiple-choice item on deterrence is reduced to a dichotomy by collapsing the three pro-deterrence categories and the two skeptical categories of the original five-point-scale. Then, there is a familiar four-fold table relating those two deterrence items (next page).

The corresponding phi is 0.31, whereas gamma equals 0.87. In contrast to phi, gamma is not sensitive to marginal distributions and may approach unity, even where marginal distributions differ. As there is a major difference in skewness of both variables here, gamma provides a much better estimate of the degree of similarity of responses than phi does. Out of 851 respondents, 589 (69%) consistently subscribe to deterrence, another 206 (24%) admit some effectiveness of deterrence without stating that deterrence is the primary cause of absence of East-West war, 9 (1%) respond somewhat inconsistently, 47 (5–6%) consistently deny that peace through fear does work. So, these data demonstrate firm, consistent, and overwhelming support for deterrence policies.

		Deterrence (means no-war between East and West) con	pro	
Deterrence (degree of effectiveness, reduced to dichotomy)	con	47	9	56
	pro	2o6	589	795
		253	598	851

The four-fold table above may highlight another problem once more. Inspite of the strong association between the two deterrence items above, the product-moment correlation phi does not do an adequate job in summarizing it, because of deflation. Or, the numerical size of such coefficients has to be interpreted with utmost caution where we suffer from asymmetric distributions. As product-moment coefficients are required in ordinary factor analysis, such caution must also be extended to our factor analysis. That is why we did not report it in any detail, and why we relied on it only as a quick and dirty mode of summarizing results.

Belief in deterrence is systematically related to other items. Take views on causes of war. Our question is: »In your opinion, which conflicts of interest are particularly closely related to risk of war? (Welche Interessengegensätze sind Ihrer Meinung nach besonders eng mit Kriegsgefahr verbunden?)" Respondents have been asked to mark at most two out of five statements, one of which refers to the security dilemma, another to territorial conflicts of interest, and a third one to economic interests. In this context, two other answers are of special importance. We see that 68.8% subscribe to: Ideology-based conflicts of interest which arise out of different political or religious systems of belief (Ideologisch begründete Interessengegensätze, die sich aus unterschiedlichen politischen oder religiösen Glaubenssystemen ergeben). This is about the same percentage as has accepted deterrence as the primary policy of war-avoidance. Moreover, ca. 53% simultaneously stress ideological causes of war and war-avoidance by deterrence.

By contrast, 17.1 percent identify as a major cause of war: "Conflicts of security interests which are produced in the first place by the arms race (Gegensätze der Sicherheitsinteressen, die durch das Wettrüsten erst erzeugt werden)." An 82.9% majority does not endorse the idea of tension-generation by an arms-buildup. Obviously, German elites are more concerned with the idea of failure of deterrence than with fear of fueling the arms race. Slightly more than 60% subscribe to deterrence *and* reject the idea of wars because of arms races.

Those who support a deterrence approach to national security do perceive a serious and deteriorating situation in Europe. Belief in deterrence correlates (gamma) 0.49 with a pessimistic assessment of the military situation in Europe today and 0.43 with a pessimistic attitude toward future developments. Our question is: "In your opinion, did the military threat against the Federal Republic by the Warsaw-Treaty Organization decrease, remain as it was, or increase? (Hat die militärische Bedrohung der Bundesrepublik durch die Warschauer Vertragsorganisation in den 70er Jahren ihrer persönlichen Meinung nach abgenommen, ist sie gleich geblieben oder ist sie größer geworden?)" A meager 8.7% say that it decreased, 36.1% can see no change, and 55.2% percieve an increased threat. About 44% simultaneously express belief in deterrence *and* perceive an increased threat, whereas ca. 23% support deterrence *and* perceive a constant threat. By implication, a two-thirds majority sees little reason for a reduced defense effort. Less than 6% simultaneously do not support the idea of war-avoidance by deterrence as well as perceive a decreased level of threat. The pattern of answers to a related question concerning likely developments in the 1980s is fairly similar and is not reported in detail.

The German elite seems well aware of the general political ramifications of deterrence. As Weede (1975a, 1976) has argued elsewhere, deterrence needs more than a military balance, if it is to be extended from deterrence between superpowers to deterrence between their blocs. In addition, it needs clear-cut demarcation of blocs or spheres of influence, somewhat limited decision-latitude for minor and middle powers in security-related affairs, and superpower leadership. A bit to our surprise, much of the German elite is ready to accept such a view and, by corollary, a somewhat subordinate role for the FRG. As seen, 62.9% approve the following proposition: "The small- and middle-sized European nations contribute to security in Europe, if they accept the leadership of their respective superpower. (Die kleinen und mittleren europäischen Länder tragen zur Sicherheit in Europa bei, wenn sie die Führungsrolle der jeweiligen Supermacht akzeptieren)." We included another fairly similar item and received more or less the same pattern of answers. In general, those who believe in war avoidance by deterrence are more ready to see West Germany subordinated to superpower, i.e. American, leadership than the minority of those who are more skeptical about deterrence.

		Minor and middle nations should accept superpower leadership		
		Yes	No	
Deterrence avoids war between East and West	Yes	366	175	541
	No	121	112	233
		487	287	774

Whereas among those who accept deterrence, there is a 2:1 ratio in favor of acceptance of superpower leadership; among deterrence skeptics the ratio is close to 1:1. The gamma correlation between both items is 0.32. While there are some who either accept deterrence or superpower preeminence, ca. 47 percent are ready to accept both. Considering the fact that the other 53% are divided among themselves, and nearly evenly, one may speculate that those 47% will dominate German policy-making.

Among academics and intellectuals, military-industrial complex or vested interest explanations of the American defense effort have produced some controversy. The German elite hardly shares such views. We asked them: "The explanation of armaments dynamics might be reduced to two shorthand formulae (Die Erklärung von Rüstungsprozessen könnte man auf zwei knappe Formeln reduzieren):

A. One arms, because one feels threatened (= other-directed armaments).
   Es wird gerüstet, weil man sich bedroht fühlt (= außengeleitete Rüstung).
B. One arms, because industries and/or bureaucracies are interested in it (= inner-directed armaments).
   Es wird gerüstet, weil Industrien und/oder Bürokratien daran interessiert sind (= innengeleitete Rüstung)".

Results show that 10% claim that only A is a proper explanation for the US defense effort, 57.4% say primarily A, i.e., more than two-thirds do not feel that military-industrial complex or vested interest explanations carry much weight in the American case. As should be expected, preference for a threat explanation of US defense efforts is correlated (gamma = 0.54) with belief in deterrence. And 54.4% approve of deterrence *and* simultaneously reject domestic explanations of US defense efforts.

By contrast, the German elite feels different about Soviet armaments. Views on that topic are hardly correlated with views on deterrence (gamma = 0.06) and our respondents are nearly evenly divided among those who primarily rely on a threat or on a domestic explanation of USSR defense efforts.

As has been amply documented above, the "Realist" majority of the German elite beliefs in ideological roots of war and the East-West-conflict, approves of deterrence, is more afraid of a deteriorating military balance than of the arms race, rejects criticism of American defense efforts, accepts a subordinate role for the FRG and is ready to improve German defenses. While 49.7% recommend a higher defense budget, 46.8% feel the present budget to be adequate. Only 3.5% favor a defense cutback, when asked: "By which measures could one keep the deterrence potential of the Federal Army at the present level? (Mit welchen Maßnahmen könnte man das gegenwärtige Abschreckungspotential der Bundeswehr erhalten?)" As to be expected, favoring a higher defense budget is correlated (gamma = 0.44) with confidence in deterrence. Many in the German elite are as ready to admit the financial consequences of their views on national security as they are ready to accept a subordinate role for the FRG or as they are ready to admit the absolutely essential US connection.

We asked them: "Which relationship *should* hold between West Europe and the

US? (Welches Verhältnis *sollte* zwischen Westeuropa und den USA bestehen?)" 88.7 percent advocate a close and continuous relationship in defense, still 74.6% advocate such a relationship in foreign policy. And both items are correlated (gamma) with attitude toward deterrence: 0.57 for defense, 0.31 for foreign policy. There is practically nobody in the German elite who favors "as little cooperation between West Europe and the US as possible": a meager 0.7% in foreign policy, and 1.6% in defense.

While the "Realist" majority of German elites is firmly committed to deterrence and the US connection, there is some skepticism towards détente-related views. As has been reported above, only 6.5% feel an atmosphere of détente to be relevant for avoidance of war among East and West. Nevertheless, German elites favor some détente-related items. Our results show that 59.2% say yes, when asked: "Should the Conference for Security and Cooperation in Europe become a permanent institution, i.e., a regional institution for mulitlateral solution of European security problems? (Sollte die Konferenz für Sicherheit und Zusammenarbeit zu einer Dauereinrichtung werden, also eine regionale Institution zur multilateralen Regelung von europäischen Sicherheitsproblemen?)" However, CSCE is much more popular among deterrence critics than among the "Realist" majority.

		pro-CSCE		
		Yes	No	
Deterrence avoids war between East and West	Yes	312	283	595
	No	190	63	253
		502	346	848

A pro-CSCE opinion is negatively correlated (gamma = −0.46) with advocacy of deterrence. Adherents of deterrence are about equally split in their opinion about CSCE with a minor edge for those favoring it, whereas there is a 3:1 majority in favor of CSCE among critics of deterrence. Therefore, CSCE seems to be a bone of contention within the "Realist" majority.

On MBFR, majority opinion is in favor of a hard line. We asked them: "Please point to an adequate Western reaction—according to your opinion—to imaginary Eastern proposals for reduction. Eastern offers refer to CSSR, GDR and Poland. Western offers cover the area of Benelux and the FRG. (Bitte nennen Sie zu den [simulierten] Reduzierungsangeboten des Ostens jeweils die von *Ihnen* für angemessen erachtete westliche Reaktion. Die Angebote des Ostens beziehen sich auf die Gebiete der CSSR, der DDR und Polens. Die Angebote des Westens beziehen sich auf die Gebiete der Benelux-Länder und der Bundesrepublik Deutschland)". While 69.8% advocate that the West offers less in return, if the East offers a 20,000 combat troop reduction, 52.6% advocate that the West offers less in return, if the East offers an immediate 5%-reduction of combat units, and 65.9% advocate that the West offers less in return, if one third of Soviet combat divisions leave Poland, East Germany, and the CSSR. The percentages of those who want to offer more in return are 4.4, 3.9, or 5.0, i.e. always quite low. Insistence on lower Western than Eastern reductions is correlated (gamma) with advocacy of deterrence: 0.44, 0.34, and 0.36.

In addition, we tried to find out about hopes to break the vicious circles of mutual security dilemmas and arms races. We asked them: "Could a unilateral Western concession at MBFR-meetings produce reactions in Eastern societies which make their elites then concede similar measures, i.e. troop reductions of their own? (Könnte eine einseitige Vorleistung des Westens bei den MBFR-Verhandlungen in den östlichen Gesellschaften Reaktionen hervorrufen, die deren Führungen dann zu ähnlichen Maßnahmen – also eigenen Truppenverringerungen – veranlassen?)" Results show 92.3% reject such an idea; those believing in deterrence more so than others (gamma = 0.64). Germans elites do not at all believe that unilateral concessions produce desirable Soviet responses. Even among the minority that is skeptical about deterrence, merely one out of six believes in the desirability of unilateral concessions.

Adherents or proponents of détente sometimes hope for a kind of functionalist approach overcoming the East-West conflict. Peace by trade is one out of such functionalist notions. We asked: "To which statement you find it easiest to agree to?

The economic cooperation between East and West increases the military security of the FRG by détente.

Economic cooperation between East and West promotes political détente; the military risk, however, remains what it was.

Economic cooperation between East and West produces additional potential for conflict, the military risks therefore increases.

(Welcher Behauptung können Sie noch am ehesten zustimmen? Die wirtschaftliche Verflechtung von Ost und West erhöht die militärische Sicherheit der Bundesrepublik durch politische Entspannung. (Oder:) Die wirtschaftliche Verflechtung von Ost und West fördert die politische Entspannung, das militärische Risiko bleibt jedoch gleich groß. (Oder:) Die wirtschaftliche Verflechtung von Ost und West schafft zusätzliche Konfliktpotentiale, das militärische Risiko nimmt also zu)."

A solid 68.4% majority does not see any impact of economic cooperation and détente on military risk. Whereas 12% can imagine a change for the worse because of economic cooperation, merely 18.6% can imagine a change for the better.[10] Skepticism about peace by trade notions is correlated (gamma = 0.51) with belief in deterrence as a means for avoiding war. Taken together with the above reported general disbelief in any détente effects, one may argue that German elites perceive détente not to be a substitute of deterrence, but rather to be a policy largely irrelevant to national security issues. Possibly, this explains why German elites accept CSCE. Whereas there are a fairly strong consensus about deterrence and its corollaries and strictly limited hopes associated with détente, there is either less consensus or less degree of conviction behind détente-related issues.

In summary, there is a solid consensus about basic foreign policy and national security issues. German elites perceive a continuing Soviet threat and see no alternative to deterrence in close and continuous cooperation with the US. They therefore accept US leadership and a limited role for the FRG and nevertheless seem ready to increase German defense expenditure. They do not believe in détente as a substitute for deterrence, in unbalanced force reductions, or in unilateral concessions as a means to overcome the arms race and the East-West conflict. In general, those who believe in deterrence are more skeptical about the value and relevance of specific détente-related measures, i.e., there exists a minority that perceives détente as a substitute for deterrence. Depending on one's political views, one may either praise the unity and coherence of a broad and "Realist" majority that more or less wants to continue West German post-war policies, or one may deplore the lack of alternatives. Returning to the item about deterrence discussed in detail above, one may note that 41.8% believe that deterrence merely decreases the risk of war, and another 6.5% utter still more skeptical opinions about deterrence. About half of our sample knows that deterrence is not a forever-lasting solution to the problem of survival. Of course, such insights do not overcome the lack of alternative. Results show 93.4% did at least attribute *some* degree of effectiveness to deterrence. There is no policy or measure where an even remotely similar majority concedes a however small but still visible degree of effectiveness. At least partly, our "Realist" consensus may be produced by a feeling of being locked-in; of not knowing where else to move.

A More Active Role for the FRG?

Whereas correlations among items loading on the first or Realism-factor generally are moderate in size, and whereas no item passes beyond a 0.65 loading on that factor, while many cluster around 0.50-loadings, the pattern of responses is much simpler, as far as the second factor is concerned. There is one clearly dominating item with a 0.93 loading: "Which role *should* the FRG take over in future, given her economic and military potential? (Welche Rolle sollte die Bundesrepublik künftig aufgrund ihres wirtschaftlichen und militärischen Potentials übernehmen?)" While 36% said "she should shoulder more foreign policy responsibility (sollte stärkere außenpolitische Verantwortung übernehmen)", 59.6% said "she should keep her level of international commitments constant (sollte das Ausmaß ihrer internationalen Verpflichtungen beibehalten)", and 3.6% said "she should reduce her foreign policy activities somewhat (sollte ihre außenpolitischen Aktivitäten etwas zurückschrauben)". Inspite of the reduction alternative being much more cautiously formulated than the increase alternative, about 10 times as many respondents prefered a more active foreign policy rather than a still lower profile for the FRG. Again, responses reveal a considerable degree of foreign policy consensus among German elites. While the majority feels that the German foreign policy profile is about right, there is some potential for more activism.

Following the general question, we asked a set of more specific questions in order to ascertain where German elites consider to take over a more active stance and by which means. While 10.2 percent argued in favor of a stronger military position of the Federal Republic in Western Europe, 34.4% did so in favor of a stronger political position of the FRG in Western Europe. Responses to both items are highly correlated (gamma) with general advocacy for an active German policy: 0.91 for defense and 0.98 for politics. Those who argue for more activism are overwhelmingly thinking of the political sphere, i.e. 85% of them, whereas merely 24% of them favor a more active defense policy.

There is much less consensus on priorities concerning the domain of policy where activities might be increased. While 21.4% favor the UN context of international peacekeeping with the important exception of German military contributions, 13.8% favor participation in UN peacekeeping including military contributions, 15.6% desire a more active "Ostpolitik", and 17.5% a more active developmental policy towards the Third World. All of these items are correlated (gamma) 0.9 or higher with general readiness to involve Germany in world affairs. Nevertheless, increased activism seems to be a minority concern. First, a close to sixty percent majority feels that the present level of activism is about right. Second, within the (slightly higher than) one-third minority that is inclined towards more activism, there never is something like a consensus on what to do. Concerning UN-related activities excluding military contributions, there are nearly as many foreign policy activists in favor of it as against. Concerning UN-related activities, including military contributions to peacekeeping, there are nearly twice as many who object to it as those who accept it even among foreign policy activists. Concerning both "Ostpolitik" and developmental policies toward the Third World, advocates of specific activism never constitute more than a 43% minority of those inclined towards activism.

In summary, most of the German elite accept the level of foreign policy activity as it is. While the minority inclined towards a more active stance is much larger than those in favor of reduced levels of activity, there nevertheless seems to be little, if any support for specific foreign policy initiatives among German elites. The strongest consensus (89.8%) refers to a refusal to to something; namely to take over a more active military role in Western Europe. The percentage of those ready to advocate specific fields for activities never surpasses 20 percent. While the (nearly) 37% who feel diffusely inclined towards some unspecified type of activism, there is no agreement at all on any specifics. Again – as with the "Realist" conceptions above – the "conservative" bias in German elite opinion may either be applauded as remarkable elite unity or as some kind of lock-in by pursuing present policies because of inabilities to think of and to agree on something different.

West European and Atlantic Bonds

The North Atlantic Community factor again lacks the simplicity of the "role for the FRG"-factor. All items concerning US – West European cooperation load somewhere close to 0.50, while those refering to intra-European cooperation load around 0.30 as far as expectations are concerned, and still lower where desires or hopes are concerned.

Let us start with US – West European relations. We asked: "Which relationship *should* exist between Western Europe and the US? (Welches Verhältnis *sollte* zwischen Westeuropa und den USA bestehen?)" The question has been posed separately for three domains of policy, and four categories have been provided for answering:

	Degree of desired collaboration (Grad der gewünschten Zusammenarbeit)			
	Close and continous (eng und kontinuierlich)	Close only in periods of crisis (eng nur in Krisenzeiten)	Merely loose cooperation (nur lose Zusammenarbeit)	As littel as possible (so wenig wie möglich)
Economic policy (Wirtschaftspolitik)	69.4	15.4	14.3	0.9
Foreign policy (Außenpolitik)	74.6	17.4	7.3	0.7
Defense policy (Verteidigungspolitik)	88.7	7.5	2.2	1.6

Obviously, the overwhelming majority of the German elite wants as strong a link between the US and West Europe as possible. For each domain of politics, a two-thirds majority votes in favor of close and continuous collaboration, reaching an eight out of nine majority where defense is concerned. Very few, indeed, desire to minimize cross-Atlantic cooperation, although those few do seem to disagree with defense cooperation more than with any other type of cooperation. Given the small absolute numbers (14) involved at this end of the distribution, however, one should not make too much of this.

As has been pointed out in a previous chapter, the desire for close cooperation between Western Europe and the US is correlated with "Realist" views about the Communist threat, the perceived need for deterrence, a stable military balance, and a readiness to accept a somewhat limited and subordinate role of the FRG to the US.

While there is a fairly broad consensus about the desirability of cross-Atlantic bonds, there is some doubt among West German elites whether the desirable will be realized.

The table of expectations for the 1980s is as follows:

	Degree of expected collaboration			
	Close and continuous	Close only in periods of crisis	Merely loose cooperation	As little as possible
Economic policy	29.6	32.8	36.1	1.6
Foreign policy	33.8	47.4	18.5	0.2
Defense policy	63.6	31.3	4.4	0.6

While there has been truly overwhelming support of the desirability of cross-Atlantic ties, expectations are more evenly divided between the first three categories. Only for the defense sphere, a close to two-thirds majority expects close and continuous collaboration. Given the correlation of German desires for Atlantic ties and perceived deterrence needs, one may conclude that this is the most important aspect of Atlantic cooperation for Germans. On the other hand, it has to be pointed out that those who expect close and continuous economic relations is down 40% compared to desires, those who expect close and continuous foreign policy relations is down 41% compared to desires, and even those who expect close and continuous defense cooperation is down 25% compared to desires. There obviously is some grave concern about Atlantic ties in German minds; some latent anxiety about future foreign policy and national security problems.

Taking expectations as expressed in our table, one may ask how plausible the combination of close and continuous defense cooperation and somewhat looser cooperation in foreign policy and economics is, in the long run. In addition to the discrepancy between desires and expectations, the pattern of expectations may become a source of concern and anxiety at a later point in time.

Moreover, German elites seem to know their desires much better than they trust in their expectations. Whereas the missing values percentage comes down to 2 or even less for desires, it is in between 6 and 7 for the expectation questions.

Given these still somewhat latent doubts and concerns about the future of Atlantic cooperation which is seen as connected with basic national security needs, one may ask whether German elites perceive an alternative to the American connection. The obvious alternative is European integration. Do German elites desire West European integration with a similar degree of intensity as they do Atlantic unity? In order to assess that, we asked them: "Which degree of integration among West European nations do you desire? (Welchen Integrationsgrad der Nationen Westeuropas wünschen Sie sich?)" Again, we differentiated between three political domains. Respondents could choose one out of three answers:

	Desired degree of integration (Grad der gewünschten Verflechtung) in percentages		
	full integration (voll integriert)	cooperation (kooperierend)	national autonomy (national-autonom)
Economics and finance (Wirtschaft und Finanzen)	56.0	41.9	2.1
Social and welfare policy (Gesellschafts- und Sozialpolitik)	36.0	51.5	12.5
Foreign and defense policy (Außen-und Verteidigungspolitik)	81.8	16.8	1.4

As with cross-Atlantic cooperation, an overwhelming majority of German elites want as close as possible collaboration in foreign and defense policy. As before, the desire for cooperation in other political domains is somewhat smaller than in defense and foreign policy. Most probably, this consensus on close defense ties with Western Europe, as well as with the United States, is related to Germany's exposed geopolitical position; its border with the Soviet bloc. Do German elites view close defense ties to Western Europe and the US as alternatives, or do they view both kinds of ties to supplement each other? The correlation (gamma) is low (0.38) and thus seems to suggest that those who favor European collaboration do not generally argue in favor for as strong an Atlantic tie. However, even gamma is misleading here – and other well known coefficients of association are even more so. Let us look at the cross-tabulation itself (next page):

Those 634 who simultaneously desire extremely close defense ties between Germany and her West European neighbors, as well as with the United States, constitute 74% of our sample. An overwhelming majority wants both: European integration and Atlantic Community. The second largest group, i.e. 117 (ca. 14%), wants as close ties as possible with the US while being content with something less for intra-European cooperation. Even when one collapses two cells from our table, those who want full European integration and some intermediate degree of cooperation with the US, constitute a much smaller minority, i.e. 44 + 13 = 57 (less than 7%). While most in the German elite simultaneously desire intra-European and cross-Atlantic ties, about twice as many, who make some difference,

	Desire for West European integration in foreign policy and defense			
	Full integration	Cooperation	National autonomy	
Close and continuous cooperation in defense with US	634	117	8	759
Close only in periods of crisis	44	18	1	63
Merely loose cooperation	13	6	0	19
As little as possible	9	2	3	14
	700	143	12	855

prefer the American over the European connection. This reminds one of an earlier finding by Deutsch et a. (1967) according to which French and Germans were still tied more closely to the US than to each other in 1964. Given Soviet military capabilities and the perceived need to counterbalance them, and the limited capabilities of British and French nuclear forces (Auton 1976), the preference for American protection over a more independent European option should be quite understandable.

Finally, one may point out that very few respondents favor anything like an independent German military posture. Even counting together all those who *either* desire as little as possible cooperation with the US *or* national autonomy in the European context *or* intermediate levels of cooperation with other Europeans and Americans, merely produces a percentage somewhere between five and six.

So far, only the foreign policy and defense aspect of desired European integration has been discussed. Collaboration in the economic and financial sphere scores second in our respondents' minds. A small majority wants full integration, while a large minority is satisfied with cooperation rather than integration. Although "markets" are second only in importance to defense, elite opinion is somewhat split about the desirability of full integration.

When moving to social and welfare cooperation within the European context, German attitudes become somewhat reserved or even defensive. Only a 36%-minority favors full integration, a small majority wants cooperation, and a small (but probably not negligibly small) minority feels that national autonomy provides the best for social and welfare policies.

In order to evaluate these data, one has to add some speculative elements to interpretation. In our opinion, German elite responses reflect national interest as defined by German elites: Defense and foreign policy ties with other European nations are essential, although not as essential as is the US connection; economic cooperation is desirable and should proceed; cooperation in social and welfare policy is less desirable. Unfortunately, we lack adequate data on whether our respondents consider such cooperation as a price to be paid in order to obtain defense cooperation, much less about what they are ready to trade against what. The only thing we do know is that desires for defense cooperation, on the one hand, and for economic or social welfare cooperation, on the other hand, are correlated (gamma): 0.70 for economics, 0.58 for social welfare.

As we did regarding cross-Atlantic ties, we asked for expectations concerning European integration.

	Degree of expected integration		
	Full integration	Cooperation	National autonomy
Economics and finance	18.3	71.0	10.7
Social and welfare policy	7.3	52.9	39.8
Foreign and defense policy	22.6	67.9	9.5

Irrespective of political domain, the majority expects future cooperation instead of full integration. Whether this reflects optimism or pessimism has to be read from a comparison of desires and expectations. In foreign policy and defense, the gap between full integration desires and expectations is a staggering 59%, in economics and finance it is still 38%, and even in social welfare it is still 29%. German elites are skeptical in their expectations about European integration. As far as economics and social welfare are concerned, this need not imply frustration. With respect to such cooperation, German elites are somewhat divided among themselves with a small majority wanting full economic integration, a small majority wanting merely cooperation in social welfare, and both majorities opposed by sizable minorities. Expectations of slow progress in these domains may merely save German elites from political controversy among themselves. The picture is different for defense, of course. Close to 82% want full integration, but 59% expect disappointment.

It is most interesting to compare discrepancies between desires and expectations for the Atlantic, as well as for the European case. While desires run ahead of expectations everywhere, Germans expect more disappointment from their fellow Europeans than from Americans – most of all in defense, where cooperation is most desperately sought by German elites. For Atlantic ties, 88.7% want close and continuous cooperation, still 63.6% expect to get it. So, a close to two-thirds mamority trusts Americans. By contrast, nearly as many, i.e. 81.8% want full defense cooperation in Western Europe, however, merely 22.6% expect to get it. Trust among Europeans seems somewhat underdeveloped. Disappointment seems to be taken for granted in intra-European affairs. Concerning foreign policy and economics, German elites again want closer cooperation across the Atlantic than they expect; the discrepancy is close to 40% in each case. For economics and European integration the comparable discrepancy is slightly lower. We feel that the difference is too small to merit substantive interpretation.

In summary, German elites strongly desire European as well as Atlantic cooperation—primarily in defense and in foreign policy. Not only is the desire for Atlantic cooperation in defense stronger than for European cooperation, German elites trust more in Americans to receive what they desire than in fellow Europeans. Again, there is a solid and broad consensus and a lack of perception of alternatives. Economic cooperation with both Europeans and Americans is desired as well; again more desired than expected. However, here Germans trust about as much in Europeans as in Americans for fulfillment of desires. While German elites are inclined not to move too fast in social welfare integration in Europe, they expect to avoid a dilemma, because they expect slow progress anyhow.

Let us close this chapter with a final remark on European versus American "options" for German foreign policy. We do not want to speculate whether such options exist in reality, or whether Germany can get American cooperation when it fails to achieve or receive European cooperation. However, if the option or even an alternative existed, there can be little doubt what German elites would choose: the US connection. Following Dahrendorf (1976) we expect this preference for the US over fellow Europeans to become stronger over time, when Eurocommunists will participate in Italian or French governments, or when the economic difficulties of Britain and Italy erode economic similarity which is a base for integration by falling behind too far. Unfortunately, our data do not cover this extremely interesting set of questions.

Hopes, Expectations and Fears

We already did discuss German desires, as well as expectations about cooperation between West Europe and America within various political domains, most of all in defense. This problem has been dealt with twice in our questionnaire. First, the problem was placed in the context of basic attitudes towards East-West relations, proposed role for the FRG, deterrence, and causes of war. Responses to items within that context have been discussed above. Second, the problem was taken up again when we systematically checked desired and expected scenarios for the next decade, in 15 questions each. Topics refer to East-West relations, relations within the Western Alliance, and relations within the Soviet bloc. Diplomatic, military and economic aspects, theoreof, are covered. And all of the items are simple trichotomies like more, constant, or less.

Again, we used a variety of techniques for data reduction or data grouping purposes: factor analysis based on product-moment as well as on gamma correlations where we applied Varimax as well as oblique rotations; multidimensional scaling; cluster analysis; and hierarchical cluster analysis. For two reasons, we avoid a detailed discussion of the adequacy and comparative advantage of those techniques if applied to trichotomous rank order data and some severely skewed distributions. First, our use of those results is largely limited to provision of an organizing principle for writing this chapter. Second, those few results which we do report are fairly independent of the technique chosen. The data may be arranged such as to imply six factors or clusters:[11] East-West relations desired, East-West relations expected, intra-Western relations desired, intra-Western relations expected, intra-Soviet bloc relations desired, and intra-Soviet bloc relations expected. What might be noted is that the military, economic, or diplomatic character of relations does not determine the grouping, whereas the East-West division and the desires vs. expectations distinctions do. By and large, responses within some grouping are fairly independent of responses within a different grouping. However, there is one notable exception: those who strongly desire better relations between East and West simultaneously and as strongly desire a further improvement of relations among Western nations; i.e. West German elites do not perceive any incompatibility between Western cooperation and better relations between East and West.[12]

Even a superficial look at German elite desires, regarding East-West relations, reveals a broad consensus. Between 73.5 and 88.7% of our respondents hope for an improvement in East-West relations, depending on the aspect of East-West relations concerned. Widely shared hopes refer to superpower arms control, while less broadly shared hopes refer to more trust in peaceful relations between East and West. One may ask why only about 3 out of 4 respondents hope for more trust in peaceful relations between the two military alliances. Frankly, we suspect that we made a mistake in wording the question. As it stands now, the question

		Desire	Expectation
US-USSR arms control	successful	88.7	13.4
	stagnation	9.2	65.1
	reversal (arms race)	2.1	21.5
US-USSR trade	increases	85.3	54.7
	stagnates	12.6	41.1
	decreases	2.0	4.1
US-USSR readiness for military conflict	decreases	83.7	14.4
	constant	14.2	67.9
	increases	2.1	17.8
NATO-WTO trust in peaceful relations	increases	73.5	11.4
	constant	22.5	63.2
	decreases	4.1	25.4
NATO-WTO readines for military conflict	decreases	79.3	14.4
	constant	18.7	68.4
	increases	2.0	17.2
EEC-COMECON institutionalized cooperation	increases	83.7	33.3
	stagnation	14.6	58.0
	decreases	1.7	8.7
EEC-COMECON trade	increases	88.4	66.1
	constant	9.9	28.2
	decreases	1.7	5.7

may be understood either primarily referring to better relations between NATO and WTO, or as primarily referring to a more trusting Western attitude. One may well hope for the former and simultaneously be skeptical about the latter. This ambiguity in the question, rather than some lack of consensus, may be behind the pattern of answers observed for this item. Similar doubts about question-wording concern the two readiness-for-military-conflict ("Konfliktbereitschaft") questions. Again, one should discern between probability of conflict and Western preparedness to meet Soviet challenges. Inspite of these flaws in our study, one may summarize that there exists an overwhelming consensus in favor of better East-West relationships, including military as well as economic affairs.

Turning to expectations, we find a different pattern. Most of the German elite expect a stalemate in attempts to improve East-West relations, at least as far as political-military affairs are concerned. About 2 out of 3 expect a stalemate at US-USSR attempts to negotiate a major arms control agreement. As many expect a constant risk of military conflict between the superpowers or the military alliances. Again as many, do not believe in the creation of more mutual trust between NATO and the Warsaw Pact. While those expecting no change are in overwhelming majority, those who expect a change for the worse consistently outnumber those who expect a change for the better. German elites are somewhat more optimistic about economic cooperation. About 2 out of 3 expect more trade between EEC and Comecon, less though still a majority between the superpowers themselves. As we learnt above, however, an overwhelming majority within the German elite does not hope for any peace dividends of trade or economic collaboration. Even where German elites are optimistic, they do not allow this optimism to carry over into national security issues.

Considering discrepancies between desires and expectations, we find that desires and expectations come fairly close to each other for economic cooperation items, i.e., ca. 30% or less difference, that they diverge ca. 50% where the institutional superstructure for EEC-COMECON cooperation is concerned, that they diverge between 60 and 75 percentage points where arms control, trust between East and West or risks of military conflict are concerned. The truly dominant source of German elite pessimism and fears is national security.

As can be seen from the next table, West German elites overwhelmingly desire improved cooperation within the Western Alliance. More than 90% support European integration, economically as well as politically. Still more than 80% support more military integration within NATO and more trade across the Atlantic. Somewhat strange is the fact that merely 17.6% desire more of an American military presence in Europe. About 2 out of 3 feel that the current level of US military presence is about right, while nearly as many Germans desire a decrease of US military presence as an increase. We did not expect this finding. Nor does it fit responses which we received from the very same people when asked a highly similar question in a different context. There, 88.7% had desired as close and continuous a cooperation as possible between the US and Western Europe in defense. Here, a meager 17.6% seem to desire more US troops. In our opinion, the small number

		Desire	Expectation
EEC-USA trade	increases	81.9	58.3
	constant	15.7	36.7
	decreases	2.4	5.0
NATO-USA US military presence in Europe	increases	17.6	9.8
	constant	65.4	49.8
	drecreases	17.1	40.5
EEC internal political integration	increases	92.2	39.0
	stagnation	6.6	54.1
	decreases	1.2	6.9
EEC internal economic integration	increases	93.2	58.5
	stagnation	5.5	36.9
	decreases	1.3	4.6
NATO internal military integration	increases	84.9	27.9
	stagnation	11.5	55.6
	decreases	3.6	16.5
COMECON internal political integration	increases	31.3	40.6
	stagnation	34.4	52.7
	decreases	34.4	6.7
COMECON internal economic integration	increases	38.8	52.5
	stagnation	35.8	42.1
	decreases	25.4	5.4
WTO internal military integration	increases	18.0	58.8
	stagnation	38.8	38.7
	decreases	43.2	2.5

of those who ask for more US presence should not be misread as indifference towards, or even alienation from, the US. We believe the overwhelming majority in favor of close and continuous cooperation reflects true desires somewhat better then the military presence item. Many respondents probably feel that present levels of US military presence are adequate for deterrence and that one cannot legitimately ask the US to shoulder an even heavier burden for the conventional defense of Western Europe. They may also feel that one should not allow desires to loose all touch with realities. Similarly, the 17.1% expressing a desire for less US military presence might confound their predictions with their desires. Admittedly, our interpretation of this findings rests on nothing more than plausibility. However, one may use a different approach to our data and come to fairly similar conclusions. In general, less than 5% and never more than a probably inflated 17% advocate a reduction of intra-Western cooperation and integration.

Turning to expectations, we find that majorities expect increases in intra-Western cooperation, i.e., more trade between US and EEC as well as within EEC. While desires for economic cooperation and trade still run ahead of expectations, at least a majority hopes to get what it wants in the economic sphere. At most, 5% expect a change for the worse, as far as Western trade is concerned. German elites are somewhat more pessimistic when it comes to political integration within EEC. Majority expectation is stagnation, although less than 7% expect a change for the worse. Turning to military integration within NATO, still a majority expects stagnation. Optimists still outnumber pessimists, but the percentage of pessimists has grown to 16.5. And there is no item where the percentage difference between those who desire and those who expect more is as high as it is with NATO military integration. A majority desires an increase and simultaneously expects stagnation. Finally, pessimism reaches a maximum on the US military presence item. More than 40% expect the US to withdraw some troops and another 50% expect a constant commitment. The percentage of optimists has fallen below ten. Optimists are outnumbered 4:1 by pessimists, in regard to US military commitment to Western Europe. In general, the West German elite consents on the desirability of as much intra-Western cooperation as possible in all domains, but it expects future achievements within the economic sphere only. It predicts stagnation within the political and military spheres and it is most concerned with the possibility of an American withdrawal from Europe.

Desires for future developments within the Soviet bloc are somewhat puzzling. We find it surprising that anybody in West Germany should desire more political, economic, or even military integration of the Communist bloc. While one may argue that Soviet bloc cohesion is as instrumental to generalized peace through fear as is Western cohesion and the balance of terror (Weede 1976), we do not want to argue that between 18 and 39% of our respondents subscribe to such a view and therefore desire more integration on the Eastern side. In order to find out, we cross-tabulated "desires" for increased Soviet bloc cohesion against the belief that acceptance of superpower guidance, by minor and middle powers in Europe, promotes peace. There is practically no relationship. Instead of looking for a substantial explanation of those findings about "desire" for Soviet bloc cohesion, one may regard those percentages as an indication of invalidity in our questions and items. However, even desires on Eastern integration make some sense. The percentage desiring less WTO military integration is higher than the percentage desiring stagnation. It is more than twice as high as the percentage of those who desire more WTO military integration, and it is higher than the percentages desiring less political or economic integration within COMECON.

Expectation data for the Soviet bloc are easier to interpret. More than half expects an increase in Soviet bloc military integration. This should be contrasted to much smaller percentages for expectations on Western military integration. And practically nobody, i.e., 2.5%, expects less Soviet bloc military integration. By contrast, 16.5% expect less military integration for NATO, and 40.5% expect a reduced level of US commitment to Western Europe. Whereas German elites expect more military integration on the Eastern side, they expect stagnation on the Western side and are concerned about US commitment. This fits well with the previously reported expectation of German elites (that security is likely to become more of a problem in the eighties than it is now).

The prospects of political integration are judged fairly similarly for COMECON and EEC. In both instances, minorities between 6 and 7% expect less, close to 40% expect more, and majorities expect neither major progress nor regression. Similarly, economic integration in the East and in the West are expected to follow a parallel course. Majorities expect more economic cooperation within the East, within EEC, and within a wider North Atlantic context, somewhere close to 40% expect stagnation and ca. 5% a reversal of integrative trends. For once, however, there is a little more optimism about likely Western achievements than about Communist ones.

In summary, broad majorities desire improved relationships between East and West. While a majority expects to get more economic cooperation, the dominant expectation on security issues is stagnation. Even worse, pessimists consistently outnumber optimists on national security issues. German elites are more optimistic on economic matters than on national security items. They desire and expect more economic cooperation with the West and they expect that Western integration in the economic sphere is unlikely to lag behind Communist-bloc integration. By contrast, military integration in the East is expected to run ahead of Western integration in the military domain, although Western successes are fervently desired. A special concern is American withdrawal from Western Europe, a prospect feared by more than 40 percent.

Partisanship and Opinion

Elites are not homogeneous, of course. First of all, elite members belong to different political parties. Or, some of the variance between elite members and their views should be related to party affiliation. As space does not permit us to analyse the full set of our items on national security according to party affiliation, we will focus on certain key items. When asked: "On what is the present situation of no-war between East and West primarily based? (Worauf beruht Ihrer Meinung nach die gegenwärtige Situation eines *Nicht-Krieges* zwischen Ost und West in erster Linie?)" 70.3% of the total sample responded by pointing to the system of military deterrence, which was one out of four suggestions. Nevertheless, this broad consensus covers some differences between parties.[13] Although supporters of deterrence form a majority within each party, majorities in some parties are overwhelming, while they are small in others. Here are the absolute numbers pro and con, as well as the percentage endorsing deterrence for each party.

	pro : con	Percentage endorsing deterrence
CSU	51 : 11	82.3
CDU	84 : 27	75.7
FDP	38 : 24	61.3
SPD	136 : 90	60.2

Whereas the Christian Democratic parties (CDU + CSU) are even more unified in support of deterrence than is elite opinion in general, Social Democrats (SPD) and Liberals (FDP) are less so.[14] While support ratios in favor of deterrence do fall neatly along some right-left continuum, one should not make too much of this because Social-Democrats and Liberals are so close to each other.

An historical account for our finding is easy. The Christian Democrats favored German rearmament in the 1950s and pressed it against Social Democratic opposition (e.g. Hanrieder 1967, Hütter 1975). While Social Democrats gradually came to accept German rearmament, NATO-membership and deterrence ca. 1960, there still seem to be some remnants of previous positions or some persisting doubts.

As military deterrence necessitates adequate defense expenditures, we should expect that Christian Democrats are more favorably disposed to increasing the West German defense budget than are the governing Social Democrats and Liberals. This is indeed what we find in our data. As there are only 3.5% of our respondents who advocate less defense spending, we will merely display absolute numbers in favor of more and constant defense spending as well as a support for higher spending ratio.

	More : Constant	Percentage endorsing higher defense expenditure
CSU	37 : 24	60.7
CDU	64 : 43	59.8
SPD	75 : 123	35.9
FDP	11 : 43	18.3

As can be seen from this table, among Christian Democrats (CDU + CSU) there are solid majorities in favor of more defense spending, whereas among Social Democrats or Liberals there is a feeling that present levels of spending are high enough. However, responses do not fall along a right-left continuum. Nobody is as skeptical of higher defense spending as the Liberals are. Moreover, within the other three parties there is much more division on this issue than there is among Liberals, where 71.7% want a constant defense budget and another 10% even want a lower one.

As Social Democrats and Liberals feel less satisfied than Christian Democrats with deterrence, it should come as little surprise that they demonstrate much more interest in détente-related measures of tension-reduction. Though only 6.5% of our total sample point to "an atmosphere of détente since the end of the cold war" as a cause for the avoidance of war, it is remarkable that only a single person from each of the Christian Democratic parties shares such a belief. Here are the absolute numbers as well as a pro-détente ratio.

	pro : con	Percentage endorsing atmosphere of détente
FDP	10 : 52	16.1
SPD	34 : 192	15.0
CSU	1 : 61	1.6
CDU	1 : 110	0.9

Believers in détente come nowhere close to being as numerous as détente-skeptics, but Christian Democrats are thouroughly unified in their skepticism, whereas Liberal and Social Democratic minorities place some hope in détente as an alternative or complement to deterrence.

As has been pointed out above, skepticism about deterrence is correlated with looking for alternatives, with hopes that détente-related policies will work in favor of peace. One such notion is "peace by trade." Again, party members differ in their evaluation. Here are absolute numbers pro and con; "con" includes no impact as well as adverse impact on peace attributed to trade.

	pro : con	Percentage endorsing peace by trade
SPD	76 : 148	33.9
FDP	20 : 41	32.8
CDU	5 : 105	4.5
CSU	2 : 60	3.2

Although believers in "peace by trade" constitute a minority everywhere, they are sizeable and possibly politically important among Liberals and Social Democrats, while they can be safely neglected among Christian Democrats.

Let us now look at the distribution of CSCE-support over parties. This item discriminates particularly well between Liberals or Socialists, on the one hand, and Christian Democrats, on the other hand. While CSCE supporters constitute majorities among Social Democrats and Liberals, they are minorities among Christian Democrats.

	pro : con	Percentage in favour of CSCE
SPD	183 : 41	81.7
FDP	46 : 14	76.7
CDU	37 : 70	34.6
CSU	15 : 45	25.0

Here, Social Democrats and Liberals and Bavarian Christian Democrats are more unified within parties than are other Christian Democrats. On other items, all Christian Democrats overwhelmingly supported deterrence and equally overwhelmingly rejected détente-related beliefs, whereas Social Democrats and Liberals supported deterrence, but with less conviction, and placed some hopes in détente notions. Christian Democrats can easily be unified behind "Realist" postures, and Liberals and Social Democrats behind measures that intend to overcome the need for Realist policies. Outside Bavaria, some détente-related issues may threaten Christian Democratic unity. (Remember, our survey had been conducted in 1976, before Carter took office and a CSCE-related human rights debate began.) By and large, however, our data seem to suggest, 1. that there is more potential for within-party conflict among Social Democrats and Liberals on national security matters than among Christian Democrats, 2. that only Liberals and Social Democrats really look for some means to overcome the deterrence deadlock.

As we previously showed, views on deterrence and détente are related to views on the necessity to continue as close as possible a defense cooperation between Western Europe and the United States. Therefore, we should expect Christian Democrats to stress this point even more heavily than Social Democrats or Liberals.

	Close : Other	Percentage endorsing close cooperation
CDU	102 : 8	92.7
CSU	57 : 5	91.9
SPD	192 : 16	86.1
FDP	49 : 7	81.7

Again, majorities in favor of "close and continuous cooperation" with the US are overwhelming everywhere, but more so among Christian Democrats than elsewhere.

Deterrence or peace through fear in Central Europe is based on the balance of terror and US military commitment to the defense of Western Europe. US commitment might have a price other than, and in addition to Western European contributions to conventional manpower. As Europeans and most of all West Germans need the US more than the US needs us, part of the price tag for US military commitment may be willing acceptance of US leadership. Somewhat to our surprise we found a general willingness to accept limited decision latitude of minor and middle nations in Europe as a positive factor in promoting peace. However, we find some differences along party lines. Here are the numbers and ratios in favor of superpower leadership acceptance:

	pro : con	Percentage endorsing superpower leadership
FDP	25 : 32	43.9
SPD	121 : 90	57.3
CSU	17 : 9	65.4
CDU	80 : 24	76.9

Christian Democrats are most ready to subordinate to superpower leadership, while Liberals are least ready to do so, while the Social Democrats and Bavarian Christian Democrats range in between. This is the second item where Liberals play a conspicuous role. Here, they are the only party where a majority does not accept limited decision latitude for Europeans including, of course, the FRG. Before, they have been identified as the party with the most critical attitude towards the defense budget. Readiness to pay some price for deterrence and peace through fear seems to be minimized among Liberals. By contrast, Christian Democrats seem to be ready to pay quite a bit for the only type of security they can perceive: deterence in cooperation with the US where the FRG is restricted to the role of a junior partner, but still has to pay for her defense.

Most difficult to interpret may be results on the advocacy for more activism in FRG foreign policy. Here, Social Democrats and Liberals and Christian Democrats outside of Bavaria seem to be more in favor of the status quo, in favor of continuing older levels of activity or inactivity.

	More active : Constant	Percentage favoring more active role
CSU	34 : 23	54.8
CDU	39 : 66	35.8
FDP	20 : 39	32.2
SPD	62 : 160	27.8

The only party where activists outnumber those who are content with present levels of activity is the Bavarian Christian Democrats. To make results even more puzzling, the percentage of those who want to decrease activities — while truly negligible everywhere — is highest among Bavarian Christian Democrats, also. Should the advocacy of activism be read as discontent with present Social Democratic and Liberal policies, or does it really mean activism, and if so, of what variety? On the one hand, Bavarian Christian Democrats belong to the staunchest supporters of deterrence and cooperation with the US and belong to the most outspoken critics of détente-related political activities. On the other hand, they ask for more — of what? We simply do not know. But activism seems to be some bone of contention among the Christian Democratic sister parties.

According to a 1972 elite survey, based on 1825 respondents, Social Democrats and Liberals agreed with each other much more on foreign policy than on managing the economy (Hoffmann-Lange 1976 p. 225). There is still no sign for an end to such a Social Democratic-Liberal consensus on foreign policy and national security. Sometimes, Liberals differ from all other parties; they are least favourably disposed toward defense expenditures and acceptance of superpower guidance.[15] As they disagree more with Christian Democrats than with Social Democrats on these topics, such a divergence of Social Democratic and Liberal opinion does not threaten the present coalition. However, there seems to be some potential for conflict within both parties along the deterrence-détente dimension. Among Christian Democrats, deterrence is safe and unifying, but activism (or generalized discontent?), as well as some détente policies like CSCE, create some potential for conflict between these parties.

Military Background and Opinion

It should come as little surprise that civilians and the military[16] differ in their evaluation of some basic foreign policy issues. The task of the military is deterrence, in order to avoid the necessity of defense. Do they believe in the effectiveness of deterrence? As we said above, an overwhelming majority of our sample believes in deterrence more than in any other means to avoid war. So does the military, however, with even more confidence. If we split our sample into two subsets, where one never has had any military experience, and where the other one is either still active or reserve or has had earlier military experience, we see that belief in deterrence, as a tool for the avoidance of war between East and West, is correlated with military experience: gamma equals 0.30. The corresponding fourfold table is:

		Military experience		
		never	some, past or present	
Deterrence avoids war between East and West	no	96	152	248
	yes	151	441	592
		247	593	840

Among those who have had some military experience, the ratio of proponents against skeptics is close to 3.0, and among "pure" civilians it is close to 1.5. Similarly, if military rank is correlated with either of our two deterrence items, we find that the higher the rank, the firmer the belief in deterrence (gammas are 0.26 and 0.21).

Deterrence presupposes adequate military strength. To maintain military forces you need money. Therefore, one might expect that the military adherents of deterrence also favor a higher, rather than constant or lower, defense budget for the FRG. Moreover, one even might conceive of the military as a type of interest group that seeks higher defense expenditures as desirable in itself. However, our data provide little support for such a view. Active military duty is but weakly related to demands for a higher defense budget (gamma = 0.18).

From the table below we can read that military as well as civilian elite are fairly evenly divided among those who deem a defense increase necessary and those who believe that present levels are still adequate. It may be of little importance that the military is slightly more in favor of a higher defense budget than others are,[17] whereas it is of more importance that slightly more than half of our respondents

	Military duty		
	No	Active	
Decrease defense budget	28	1	29
Constant defense budget	281	92	373
Increase defense budget	282	116	398
	591	209	800

favor increased defense spending with less than four percent arguing for defense cuts. Other background variables, such as military experience (gamma = 0.16) or military rank (gamma = 0.18), also show little relationship with advocacy of more defense spending.

Few German elite members believe in an atmosphere of détente as a means for the avoidance of war. And those who do, are likely to never have had any experience with military service. Belief in the effectiveness of an atmosphere of détente is negatively correlated (gamma = −0.40) with military experience.

		Military experience		
		never	some, past or present	
Atmosphere of détente helps to avoid war	no	222	566	788
	yes	25	27	52
		247	593	840

Of course, those who argue in favor of détente are tiny majorities in all groups and never more than 1 out of 10. But among those with some military experience they are close to 1 out of 20 only. The correlation (gamma) between military rank and belief in an atmosphere of détente, as a means to avoid war, is about as high and negative (−0.39).

Another alternative to deterrence might be the functionalist approach, i.e., attempts to increase military security by economic cooperation between East and West. While most elite members, whatever the military or civilian background, assume that economic cooperation neither increases nor decreases military security, "pure" civilians, nevertheless, place more hope in peace by trade than those with some military background.

	Military experience		
	never	some, past or present	
East-West-Trade decreases security	18	82	100
East-West-Trade doesn't affect security	156	420	576
East-West-Trade increases security	71	86	157
	245	588	833

The correlation (gamma) between belief in "peace by trade" and military experience is negative (−0.36). Whereas, those who never have had any military experience, give much more credibility to more security because of trade than to the opposite statement, those with some military experience find increasing risks about as plausible as decreasing risks coming with trade. The correlation (gamma) between military rank and belief in peace by trade.is similar in sign and magnitude (−0.29).

As far as CSCE is concerned, the military hardly differs from general elite opinion. Some military experience is negatively correlated (gamma = −0.13) with a positive attitude towards CSCE, and so is military rank (gamma = −0.27). Again, the military displays even less confidence in détente-related measures than the elite in general, although differences are less marked here than elsewhere.

As we have seen, the military feels even more positive about deterrence and even less positive about détente than German elites in general. Deterrence works in a North Atlantic framework, much of it — if not most of it — is provided by the United States. The military fully appreciates this fact and argues even more strongly in favor of a continuing US connection in defense than do other groups. Active military duty is highly correlated (gamma = 0.71) with a desire for as close and continuous a defense relationship as possible between Western Europe and the US.

No-one in the military would like to miss US cooperation in periods of crisis, nearly everybody likes to see it as closely as possible. Among civilians, as among the military, an overwhelming majority favors the highest possible degree of defense cooperation between Western Europe and the US. But, whereas 14% of all civilians feel that as close as possible is unnecessary, less than 3% of the active military share such a view.

Desired cooperation West Europe - US	Active military duty		
	No	Yes	
As little as possible	14	0	14
Merely loose cooperation	18	0	18
Close only in periods of crisis	56	6	62
Close and continuous	531	208	739
	619	214	833

In general, the correlation between military background variables and opinions is maximized if we dichotomize military experience in such a way as to compare groups with some (past or present) military experience against those with none at all. Concerning US-West European defense cooperation, it is different. While some military experience correlates (gamma) 0.39 with desire for US-European defense cooperation, active military service correlates much higher, i.e., 0.71 as reported above. Obviously, it is daily experience within the NATO framework, rather than some familiarity with military affairs, that reinforces pro-Atlantic attitudes. And the higher the military rank, the greater the desire to continue American-European defense links (gamma = 0.37).

Deterrence plus US connection implies a somewhat subordinate role for US allies in Europe. We included two items on willing acceptance of superpower guidance or limited decision-latitude for Europeans. Military rank correlates (gamma) 0.33 or 0.30 with these items. Active military duty correlates lower; gamma equals 0.10 or 0.17. Some military background, whether past or present, means more willing acceptance of a subordinate role for the FRG; gamma equals 0.29 or 0.36. Therefore military experience as well as military rank increase the willingness to play a secondary role.

Finally, we may compare military and civilians in their willingness to support a more active role for the FRG. Here, there is practically no difference between military and civilians, whether we compare those with some and those with no military experience, whether we compare active duty and other, and whether we group according to military rank. The highest correlation (gamma) we ever got between some military background variable and proposed FRG activities is 0.02.

In summary, military background, whether rank, experience, or active duty, generally reinforces a belief in deterrence, a desire for cooperation in defense with the US, an acceptance for present levels of activity of the FRG in foreign policy, an acceptance of a subordinate role for the FRG, and skepticism about détente-related measures. It should come as little surprise, that military background reinforces "Realism" rather than Idealism. But military rank and active duty also reinforce insights in limited German decision-latitude. Nobody surpasses the German military in NATO-loyalty. We did not find any opinions that permit an interpretation along the lines of a nationalistic military; quite to the contrary.

If one relates the military-civilian background dimension to partisan attitudes, one cannot escape the conclusion that the military is closer in its attitudes to Christian Democrats than to Social Democrats or Liberals. Like Christian Democrats, the military expresses particularly firm belief in deterrence, the US connection and special skepticism about détente-related measures. However, there is one issue where the German military is closer to Liberals, Social Democrats, Christian Democrats (CDU only), on the one hand, than to Bavarian Christian Democrats (CSU), on the other hand. The Bavarian desire for a more active FRG finds no military echo inspite of general concordance of views on the Realism-Idealism or Deterrence-Détente dimension.

In general, there is a "Realist" or deterrence consensus within the German elite. Such a consensus is even stronger in the military or among those with military experience. The political and defense status quo finds its institutional home in the German armed forces.

Critics of "Realist" views in foreign policy might suspect that military service reinforces authoritarian attitudes and that "Realist" views are part of an authoritarian attitude syndrome. Though we did not investigate authoritarianism, research of other social scientists permits us to cast considerable doubt on such an interpretation. A panel study of 1037 West German conscripts demonstrates that authoritarian attitudes are actually decreased during military service (Roghmann and Sodeur 1972). Moreover, as strong an anti-authoritarian effect, due to college education, cannot be observed. Similar findings on military experience and attitudes toward authority for the US have been reported by Campbell and McCormack (1957). While the explanation of military "Realism" by military authoritarianism should be rejected as implausible, a recent American study on "the effect of military service on political attitudes" provides an alternative cue. According to Jennings and Markus (1977), military service raises attention for international, geopolitical, and cosmopolitan affairs. Again, college education does not produce a similar effect. Possibly, the strength of "Realist" or pro-deterrence consensus among the West German military might be related to, or even be explained by, more careful attention to problems of national security within, rather than outside of, the military.

Deviant and Divided Elites:

Foreign Policy or Peace Researchers and Trade Unions

As we analyze an accidental sample, utmost caution is required. Readers should keep that in mind when reading this chapter. Our subsample of foreign policy or peace researchers[18] poses some special problems. It contains only 57 persons. It is somewhat heterogeneous in at least two important ways: From channel of access we know that some of them are identified as peace researchers by position or participation, e.g. in the "Working Group for Peace and Conflict Research (AFK)" or in the "Hessen Institute of Peace and Conflict Research (HSFK)", whereas others belong to somewhat more established and possibly more traditional institutions like the "German Society for Foreign Policy (DGAP)". Of course, some of them are to be found within universities, too. While we considered the option to treat foreign policy researchers separately from peace researchers, we decided not to do so, because resulting numbers of cases would become too small and any such distinction would be difficult, arbitrary, and largely tautological.

Moreover, the term "researchers" does not apply to all of our foreign policy or peace researchers equally well. Merely 14 of them have completed their "Habilitation" and another 23 their Ph.D. (Dr.). While we considered the possibility of calling them only "researchers", we dismissed such a procedure as we wanted to avoid losing cases. Moreover, those who have not finished their Ph.D. still might reflect the intellectual atmosphere in their respective institutions. They soon might become full members of the research community. That is why we did not even eliminate those seven persons who have not yet finished even the equivalent of an M.A. degree.

Our foreign policy or peace researchers group is biased in some important ways. While 18 belong to the Social Democratic Party, merely 4 identify themselves with the Christian Democrats. Moreover, being a foreign policy or peace researcher is correlated with being a union member (gamma = 0.37). While less than one fourth of the total sample claims union membership, as much as 40% of our foreign policy or peace researchers do. Three out of four of our foreign policy or peace researchers never experienced any military service, whereas 70 percent of our total sample have served at some time with the military.

The trade union[19] subsample poses less problems. It is much larger. While we do not know to which unions many members belong, there is reason to assume that most of them belong to public employee's unions like ÖTV. As trade unions and foreign policy or peace researchers share many queries about status quo policies in national security affairs and foreign policy, they are treated together in this chapter.

Whereas elite opinion in general has achieved an overwhelming consensus on deterrence and related policies, union opinion seems divided. Union membership is negatively correlated with belief in deterrence (gamma = −0.40).

		Union membership		
		Yes	No	
Deterrence avoids war between East and West	Yes	113	494	607
	No	90	167	257
		203	661	864

There are nearly as many opponents to, as there are supporters of, deterrence within unions — very much in contrast to general elite opinion. Being a foreign policy or peace researcher also is negatively correlated (gamma = −0.32) with confidence in deterrence.

		Being a foreign policy or peace researcher		
		Yes	No	
Deterrence avoids war between East and West	Yes	32	575	607
	No	25	232	257
		57	807	864

Similar to union elites and in contrast to general elite opinion, foreign policy or peace researchers are divided among themselves on deterrence. If we turn to the other deterrence item which evaluates effectiveness on a five-category scale, union membership and belief in deterrence effectiveness correlate (gamma) −0.45, being a foreign policy or peace researcher and belief in deterrence effectiveness −0.51. Therefore, skepticism and within-group division on deterrence seem to be consistent over items.

Those who are skeptical about deterrence should not be expected to be particularly enthusiastic about the defense budget. This is, indeed, what we find. Union membership is negatively correlated (gamma = −0.40) with a positive attitude towards more defense spending.

While the West German elite in general is about equally divided among those who want a higher defense budget and those who merely want to keep current levels of spending, union members clearly resist the idea of still higher defense

	Union membership		
	Yes	No	
Increase defense budget	63	345	408
Constant defense budget	107	277	384
Decrease defense budget	15	14	29
	185	636	821

spending. Outside unions, higher spending advocats outnumber proponents of constant and decreasing defense budgets combined; within unions, merely one third is ready to pay more for defense. Being a foreign policy or peace researcher also is negatively correlated (gamma = −0.34) with readiness to support higher defense expenditures.

	Being a foreign policy or peace researcher		
	Yes	No	
Increase defense budget	20	388	408
Constant defense budget	21	363	384
Decrease defense budget	11	18	29
	52	769	821

What accounts for the negative correlation between being a foreign policy or peace researcher and support of defense spending, is the conspicuously high number of those foreign policy or peace researchers who actually want defense cuts. Of course, absolute numbers are extremely small — and interpretation therefore is hazardous — but those who actually want to cut into West Germany's defenses seem more likely to be found at universities or research institutions than elsewhere. In general, the media[20] do not differ from other elite opinion. With respect to defense expenditure, they do. Working for the media is negatively correlated (gamma = −0.31) with support for defense.

	Media		
	Yes	No	
Increase defense budget	15	393	408
Constant defense budget	32	352	384
Decrease defense budget	0	29	29
	47	774	821

While no-one in our media sample favors less spending, there is a 2:1 majority against more spending within the media. If one considers the impact of trade unions, the foreign policy or peace research community and media resistance to higher defense spending in combination, one may well feel that it is a tough job to convince the public of the necessity to increase spending if such necessity were to arise in order to counterbalance the increasing capabilities of the Soviet Union. The media may spread doubts[21], foreign policy or peace researchers as scientists may legitimate or rationalize them, and unions may provide muscle and voters for such a conceivable "resistance" movement.

Those who are less satisfied with official (i.e., deterrence-related) handling of national security affairs, have some incentive to look elsewhere. A major attempt to complement or supplant deterrence is détente. Few respondents, indeed, believe in détente, but trade unionists more so than others. Being a unionist is correlated (gamma = 0.57) with a belief in an atmosphere of détente as a primary factor for the avoidance of war.

		Union membership		
		Yes	No	
Atmosphere of détente avoids war	Yes	28	28	56
	No	175	633	808
		203	661	864

While still less than 1 out of 7 in the union elite believe in an atmosphere of détente as a major peace factor, non-members are still more skeptical. There, 1 out of 24 share such hopes. Foreign policy or peace researchers share the détente inclination of unionists, but less strongly so, as far as this particular item is concerned. Being a foreign policy or peace researcher is correlated (gamma = 0.37) with support for an atmosphere of détente.

		Being a foreign policy or peace researcher		
		Yes	No	
Atmosphere of détente avoids war	Yes	7	49	56
	No	50	758	808
		57	807	864

While 1 out of 8 foreign policy or peace researchers places definite hopes in an atmosphere of détente, less than 1 in 16 other elite members do!

Union elites and foreign policy or peace researchers express themselves much more favorably than others on East-West trade and its security benefits. Being a union member is correlated (gamma = 0.50) with beliefs in "peace by trade".

	Union membership		
	No	Yes	
Trade decreases security	97	7	104
Trade doesn't affect security	461	130	591
Trade increases security	96	65	161
	654	202	856

An absolute majority of union-members, as well as of others, does not believe in any systematic relationship between trade and peace. However, the majority is somewhat smaller among unionists than elsewhere. Moreover, there are many more union members who believe in security benefits of trade than in the opposite, whereas non-members come close to being evenly divided. Foreign policy or peace researchers seem to be about as optimistic on this topic as unions. Being a foreign policy or peace researcher is correlated (gamma = 0.51) with belief in peace by trade.

	Being a foreign policy or peace researcher		
	No	Yes	
Trade decreases security	100	4	104
Trade doesn't affect security	564	27	591
Trade increases security	135	26	161
	799	57	856

In remarkable contrast to general elite opinion, there are nearly as many foreign policy or peace researchers who believe in a peace dividend of trade as there are those who do not believe in any security effects of economic cooperation and trade. Obviously, foreign policy or peace researchers have a different image of the working of world politics from the rest of the German elite.

Another détente item refers to the CSCE. Being a union member is strongly correlated with CSCE (gamma = 0.67).

		Union membership		
		No	Yes	
CSCE should be institutionalized	No	314	32	346
	Yes	333	169	502
		647	201	848

Whereas elites outside unions are fairly evenly divided on this issue, there is an overwhelming majority in support of CSCE within unions. Being a foreign policy or peace researcher is also related to CSCE, but remarkably less so; gamma is merely 0.10. And foreign policy or peace researchers are nearly as divided on CSCE as elites in general are.

In their evaluation of the arms race, political parties, civilians and military did not differ so much from each other. But union members and even more so foreign policy or peace researchers feel concerned. Union membership correlates (gamma = 0.30) with a belief that the arms race creates conflicts of interest and, thereby, is a major cause of war.

		Union membership		
		No	Yes	
Arms race leads to war	No	563	153	716
	Yes	98	50	148
		661	203	864

Those deeply concerned about the arms race constitute a minority everywhere. Being little more than 1 out of 7 among non-union members, they count for little outside. Coming close to 1 out of 4 within unions, such a minority is probably large enough not to be neglected. Foreign policy or peace researchers are even more concerned about the arms race than union elites are. Being a foreign policy or peace researcher correlates (gamma) 0.45 with such concern.

		Being a foreign policy or peace researcher		
		No	Yes	
Arms race leads to war	No	678	38	716
	Yes	129	19	148
		807	57	864

Fully, 1/3 of all foreign policy or peace researchers asked, said that arms races are a primary cause of war. As a policy of deterrence is always prone to fueling the arms race, it should come as little surprise that foreign policy or peace researchers not only place less confidence in deterrence and more in détente than others do, but also fear counterproductive effects of traditional efforts to achieve peace along "si vis pacem, para bellum" lines.

As should be expected, trade unions and foreign policy or peace researchers are less enthusiastic about North Atlantic defense ties than other elite groups. Union membership and such skepticism is correlated (gamma) 0.39.

Desired degree of defense cooperation between West Europe and US	Union membership		
	No	Yes	
Close and continuous	597	163	760
Close merely in periods of crisis	45	19	64
But loose cooperation	9	10	19
As little as possible	6	8	14
	657	200	857

The relationship is not particularly strong, but it indicates that some union members, i.e., ca. 1 out of 6, have stronger reservations against close and continuous ties in defense across the Atlantic than non-members. However, if there is a group with strong reservations it is not unionists, but foreign policy or peace researchers. Being a foreign policy or peace researcher correlates strongly (gamma = 0.74) with reservations about the American connection.

Desired degree of defense cooperation between West Europe and US	Being a foreign policy or peace researcher		
	No	Yes	
Close and continuous	726	34	760
Close merely in periods of crisis	57	7	64
But loose cooperation	14	5	19
As little as possible	3	11	14
	800	57	857

Nine out of ten, who are not foreign policy or peace researchers, desire the closest possible defense link between the US and West Europe, while merely 6 out of 10 foreign policy or peace researchers do. Foreign policy or peace researchers constitute the only group where a real division of opinion about the desirability of the US connection in defense exists, although even among foreign policy or peace researchers, pro-Americans or Atlanticists are still a majority.

German elites, in general, not only favor a close US connection, but also accept a somewhat limited and subordinate role for the FRG. Trade unions somewhat depart from that consensus. Union membership is negatively correlated (gamma = −0.31) with willing acceptance of superpower guidance for the sake of peace.

		Union membership		
		No	Yes	
Minors should accept superpower guidance	No	195	92	287
	Yes	390	97	487
		585	189	774

While there is a 2 out of 3 majority in favor of superpower guidance outside unions, union members come fairly close to an even division. Foreign policy or peace researchers find superpower guidance, and implicitly bipolarity, even harder to swallow. Being a foreign policy or peace researcher correlates (gamma) −0.58 with acceptance of superpower guidance.

		Being a foreign policy or peace researcher		
		No	Yes	
Minors should accept superpower guidance	No	253	34	287
	Yes	470	17	487
		723	51	774

While there is a two-thirds majority in favor of willing acceptance of superpower guidance in German elites in general, there is an equally strong majority against such guidance among foreign policy or peace researchers. Similar results were obtained from a related item focusing on sovereignty and independence of minors. Once again, the media join foreign policy or peace researchers and unions in their rejection of superpower guidance. In our opinion, these results may be interpreted as cues demonstrating a preference for national decision-latitude and mulitpolarity among foreign policy or peace researchers, media, and to a somewhat lesser degree among unions. This preference is not equaled among the general elite public which is ready to accept the still bipolar distribution of military power and its political corrollaries.

While foreign policy or peace researchers and unions depart somewhat from elite consensus on deterrence items or the desirability of defense connections with the US, there is no stronger desire for FRG foreign policy activism within these groups than outside. Union membership correlates (gamma) 0.10, being a peace researcher 0.02 with such activism.

Trade unions and foreign policy or peace researchers somewhat differ from other German elites. They are more critical of deterrence and the US connection and more enthusiastic about détente than others are. They are most different in their views from more conservative groups, i.e., the military and the Christian Democrats. Why? A possible explanation is that unionists and foreign policy or peace researchers do not share responsibility[22] for national security affairs, and that unions and foreign policy or peace researchers constitute segments which interact less with other and more responsible, or more directly influential, groups. In order to find out, we may cross-tabulate professional concern with national security against belonging to the foreign policy or peace research and union groupings.

		Union membership		
		yes	no	
Professional concern about national security	yes	99	386	485
	no	1o2	275	377
		201	661	862

		Being a foreign policy or peace researcher		
		yes	no	
Professional concern about national security	yes	26	459	485
	no	30	347	377
		56	806	862

Being a union member correlates (gamma) −0.18 with our dichotomized concern variable and −0.17 with the original four-category-concern scale. Being a foreign policy or peace researcher correlates −0.21 with the dichotomized as well as with the four-category concern variable. That is, our deviant and divided groups are professionally somewhat less concerned with national security than is the rest of our elite sample. Whereas, among our elites, those who are professionally concerned with national security consistently outnumber "laymen", laymen constitute bare majorities among union members and foreign policy or peace researchers. It is surprising that foreign policy or peace researchers feel less concerned about national security than others do! Unfortunately, there is no way to find out whether this difference is due to inadequate sampling within these groups or to lower level of professional concern.

The criticism leveled by foreign policy or peace researchers and union members against deterrence and the US connection as well as the détente support should not be over-valued. First, and foremost, these critical groups are divided within themselves on most details and oppose a solid, broadly based, and overwhelming consensus. Nevertheless, their nuisance potential is considerable. Some of them being university teachers, foreign policy or peace researchers may share some responsiblity for the negative attitude towards the West German army among better educated youth (Fleckenstein and Schössler 1973, p.44). The resistance potential of unions, foreign policy or peace researchers, and media against more defense spending is to be taken extremely serious. On this item, deviant elites are more unified than elites in general which are divided among those who want more and those who want a constant defense budget.

Young versus Old

A comparison of views of older and younger elite members is meaningful because discrepancies, if found, may be used for predictive purposes. The young are likely to outlast their elders and finally to replace them in positions of authority. If their views systematically differ — and if one further assumes that their views will not change towards the views of their elders, and the more so, the closer they come to top positions — then one should expect changes in the general elite opinion to be a consequence of generation replacement. By and large, our data contain little opinion differences related to age. We will report only those few instances where at least some discrepancies between young and old may be detected. For simplicity's sake, we dichotomized our age variable between 45 and 46 years. This split results in a fairly even distribution of "young" and "old".

In general, younger and older respondents do not differ significantly in their views on deterrence, defense budget, or proposed role for the FRG. However, there are some discrepancies at the détente pole of the deterrence-factor. One such item refers to peace dividends to be derived from increased East-West cooperation in economics and trade.

	Age		
	young (≤ 45)	old (≥ 46)	
East-West trade decreases security	33	65	98
East-West trade doesn't affect security	291	285	576
East-West- trade increases security	92	68	160
	416	418	834

The correlation (gamma) between age and belief in peace by trade is −0.24; i.e., the younger ones are far more optimistic about trade and economic cooperation. Of course, among young and old ca. 2 out of 3 feel that trade and military security are independent of each other. However, the viewpoint held by the other third differs. Here, the older respondents are equally split among those who hope for peace by trade and those who even expect a deterioration of the security situation because of more trade, whereas among the young the optimists outnumber the pessimists 3:1

Similar results are obtained, when one turns to the CSCE item. Age and a favorable attitude toward CSCE are negatively correlated (gamma = −0.22).

		Age: young	Age: old	
CSCE should be institutionalized	no	145	190	335
	yes	266	225	491
		411	415	826

Among both age groups, a majority favors CSCE institutionalization. This majority, however, is much more comfortable among younger than among older respondents. The latter come quite close to an even split on this issue.

As has been reported above, ca. 2 out of 3 German elite members accept the general principle that minor and middle nations in Europe — and, by implication, the FRG — should accept superpower guidance for the sake of peace. Acceptance of this principle is correlated (gamma = 0.24) with age.

		Age: young	Age: old	
Minors should accept superpower guidance	no	162	118	280
	yes	218	258	476
		380	376	756

Again, a firm majority of both age groups is ready to agree with superpower guidance. However, among the older ones, close to 70% agree, and among the younger ones merely 57%. For the younger ones superpower guidance seems to taste more bitter than for their elders.

Finally, young and old somewhat differ in their attitudes toward US-European defense links. Skepticism about defense ties and age is negatively correlated (gamma = −0.35).

Desired degree of defense cooperation between West Europe and US	Age		
	Young	Old	
Close and continuous	356	385	741
Close merely in periods of crisis	37	25	62
But loose cooperation	14	4	18
As little as possible	11	3	14
	418	417	835

Within the total sample, positive attitudes toward military cooperation with the US are overwhelming. So they are within both age groups. However, among older respondents, those who desire something less than close and continuous cooperation, clearly fail to constitute even a ten percent minority, whereas among younger ones the ten percent mark is easily surpassed.

In summary, age differences have minor impact on attitudes toward national security and foreign policy questions. For some central issues, like evaluation of deterrence or proposed role for the FRG, age differences are virtually absent. Minor discrepancies exist, as far as détente-related policies and German-American ties are concerned. The young are somewhat more optimistic about the chances to contribute to peace by economic cooperation or about CSCE. The young are less ready to accept superpower guidance and they less strongly desire close and continuous defense cooperation with the US. However, one should not make too much out of those differences. First, they are minor in magnitude. In general, the young support the broad German foreign policy consensus overwhelmingly, even if less overwhelmingly than their elders. Second, even if larger discrepancies in opinions toward national security items were to be found, this in itself would imply little basis for foreign policy change. There is nothing to prevent an even greater assimilation of attitudes among the young to those of older respondents, when younger ones get older and move up the hierarchy. Whether this happens or not, may be an interesting general social science problem, but is of little concern here. There just seems to be no biological basis for predicting visible change in West German elite opinion.

The Second Wave or Data from Spring 1977

We experienced some major problems with our second wave. First of all, panel mortality has been high. While we had 864 respondents in the first wave, we came down to 258 in the second one, i.e., we lost ca. 70% of our sample. Partly, this extremely high rate is due to bureaucratic interference within the department of defense and the armed forces. Another part thereof is self-selection, of course. However, panel mortality does not indicate lack of enthusiasm about the project among respondents. Many second wave participants volunteered to take part in third, and later waves, as well as to ask friends and colleagues to participate.

As we found so much consensus in the first wave, we should not even expect feedback of first-wave results to have major impact. Presumably, many of our respondents have been aware of existing consensus, though probably not of its scope, even before we confirmed such an expectation. Moreover, being told that most others feel like yourself is not likely to make you change your own opinion. So, by and large, the second wave of our survey reinforces results from the first one.

The table below permits two comparisons. First, we may compare opinions in 1976 and 1977 for those who answered our questionnaire both times. Such a comparison demonstrates that change has been minor, but in favor of Realist or deterrent policies. Threat perception is slightly up. Confidence in deterrence is still growing. Readiness to pay more for defense is growing. Expectation and desire for close defense cooperation between West Europe and the United States is still higher and so is willingness to accept superpower leadership. Open-ended questions in the 1977 survey provide some cue for the reasons behind this minor change; respondents feel threatened by continuing Soviet efforts to further increase their military superiority in Central Europe as well as by Soviet power politics on a global scale as demonstrated in Angola. Hopes in détente as a means to achieve peace have been largely abandoned. There are only two items where change is in favor of détente related policies. CSCE support is up. However, since Carter started his vigorous human rights campaign, and since Soviet bloc dissidents use this point to criticize the regime, even endorsement of CSCE in 1977 might mean something different from such an endorsement in 1976. Moreover, the increase in support for peace by trade is negligible. So, change seems to imply a further consolidation of Realist consensus on deterrence in close and continuous cooperation with the US. Finally, the desire for a more active role of the FRG has also grown.

Another comparison refers to possible effects of sampling bias. Above, we admitted three types of bias in our elite sample. Firstly, bias in favor of the military, secondly, bias against (non-Bavarian) Christian Democrats, thirdly, bias against topmost elites. Only the latter bias covers both waves to an equal degree. In the first wave, we had ca. 25% active military, in the second one we came down to

	Percentage of endorsement		
	1976 Data (N = 864)	(N = 258)	1977 Data (N = 258)
Deterrence avoids war between East and West	70.3	69.4	75.6
Threat from WTO in 1980s is expected to grow	55.3	51.2	53.8
FRG defense budget should go up	49.7	48.0	52.2
Close and continuous defense cooperation between US and West Europe desireable	88.7	85.0	89.9
(expected)	(63.6)	(63.1)	(69.4)
Minor and middle powers should accept superpower leadership	62.9	61.3	66.5
Peace by trade	18.8	17.8	18.2
Peace because of atmosphere of détente	6.5	8.9	2.7
CSCE should be institutionalized	59.2	58.9	66.1
More active role for FRG	36.7	36.7	39.7

15%. Or, there is much less of a military bias in the second wave compared to the first one. In the first wave, 28.5% of those answering the party membership question said they were Social Democrats, whereas merely 21.8% identified themselves with either of the two Christian Democratic sister parties. In the second wave, the percentage of Social Democrats is still higher (32.5%) and the percentage of Christian Democrats still lower (19.4%). While pro-military bias is reduced in the second wave compared with the first one, anti-Christian Democratic bias is strengthened in the second wave. Most commentators on West German politics would therefore say that the second wave is somewhat to the left of the first one. Let us see whether such a shift has any sizable impact on results.

If our smaller 1977 sample is somewhat to the left of our larger 1976 sample, then we may use comparisons of all 1976 data against 1977 data or against a subsample of 1976 data as instruments to get some feeling for the robustness of our findings against sampling bias. Whether you compare the 258 person subsample and the total sample from 1976 or the 1976 and 1977 samples, there are few truly interesting differences. Within 1976, subsample and total sample rarely differ by even 2%. Where they do, results are compatible with our feeling that the subsample is to the left of the total sample, because the subsample feels less threatened by WTO, desires cooperation with the US less strongly, and places more hopes in an atmosphere of détente. Most of the difference between 1976 and 1977 data is due to change. As we indicated before, change tends to reinforce the existing pro-deterrence consensus. As there are no truly major differences between samples or subsamples, and the largest differences to be found are related to change, we are confident that sampling bias has little impact on our major finding: firm and stable pro-US and pro-deterrence consensus.

What About Individual Change?

In the last chapter we found that elite opinion in general did not change much between 1976 and 1977. Nevertheless, such a result may cover substantial change of opinions among individuals. That is why we present a more detailed comparison below. Depending on the item considered, gamma varies between 0.54 and 0.89. As these correlations are less than perfect, there has been some change. A still simpler way to describe the amount of change is to find out how many hold stable views and how many experience any change of opinion. As can be seen from the table below, at least 64.8% held constant opinions, while this number went up to 91.5% for some items. Typically, about 3 out of 4 persons did not change, whereas one did. Of course, some of the change is spurious and due to measurement error, possibly even to respondents "answering" questions in a random manner.

	Gamma correlation between 76 and 77 responses	Percentage giving exactly the same response both times
Deterrence avoids war between East and West	0.75	76.0
Threat from WTO in 1980s is expected to grow	0.68	65.3
FRG defense budget should go up	0.80	72.0
Close and continuous defense cooperation between US and West Europe desirable	0.77	84.6
(expected)	(0.54)	(64.8)
Minor and middle powers should accept superpower leadership	0.87	80.1
Peace by trade	0.89	78.4
Peace because of atmosphere of détente	0.88	91.5
CSCE should be institutionalized	0.87	78.6
More active role for FRG	0.82	76.2

Where N is between 226 and 258, it depends on the number of missing values.

Whether you look at gamma or at percentage of no change, expectations about defense cooperation between US and West Europe and evaluations of WTO threat, have been most subject to change. The story behind these changes is different. For defense cooperation expected between US and West Europe, nearly all change is due to respondents expecting more cooperation. While there has been quite a bit of individual change on perception of WTO threat, there is little of a sample-wide trend. For two other less stable items, i.e., deterrence and FRG defense budget, individual change had some effect on marginal distributions. Positive evaluations of deterrence increased from 69.4 to 75.6%; positive attitudes to defense spending from 49.1 to 53.4%. As we pointed out in the last chapter, most changes that did occur, strengthened pro-deterrence and Atlanticist consensus.

	Gamma correlation between 76 and 77 responses			Percentage giving exactly the same responses in 76 and 77		
	Unions	Foreign policy or peace research	Both combined	Unions	Foreign policy or peace research	Both combined
Deterrence avoids war between East and West	0.64	0.83	0.71	68.1	76.7	71.1
Threat from WTO in 1980s is expected to grow	0.42	0.60	0.48	56.9	46.1	55.9
FRG defense budget should go up	0.76	0.78	0.81	71.9	64.0	70.9
Close and continuous defense cooperation between US and West Europe desireable	0.83	0.93	0.89	80.6	83.3	84.0
(expected)	(0.44)	(0.76)	(0.49)	(60.8)	(60.0)	(61.5)
Minor and middle powers should accept superpower leadership	0.91	1.00	0.91	81.7	83.4	80.6
Peace by trade	0.91	0.88	0.92	77.6	78.6	78.8
Peace because of atmosphere of détente	0.81	1.00	0.82	81.2	90.0	81.9
CSCE should be institutionalized	0.91	0.63	0.90	88.2	67.8	85.1
More active role for FRG	0.62	0.96	0.69	72.7	84.6	75.4

Where the number of union members varies between 57 and 69; foreign policy or peace researchers between 24 and 30, it depends on missing values.

Our main interest in this chapter is to investigate possible effects of feedback of information. Remember that first wave respondents have been offered a booklet of tables with responses from the entire sample as a reward for filling out our questionnaire. As only those respondents got this information who provided us with their addresses, we assume that most of them actually looked at first wave results. If they did, did it change opinions of their own? By and large, 3 out of 4 did not change. Moreover, some changes almost certainly are not due to feedback of information. As said before, we should not expect much change from those who learn that others feel much the way they do. What about the two most deviant groups in our study, trade union members and foreign policy or peace researchers? Let us look first to both subsamples combined. Gamma varies between 0.48 and 0.92 compared with 0.54 and 0.89 for the entire 1977 sample. The percentage giving exactly the same response varies between 55.9 and 85.0% for the foreign policy or peace researchers plus trade union members subsample compared with 65.3 and 91.5% for the entire 1977 sample. At least some items are somewhat less stable among unions and foreign policy or peace researchers than elsewhere. Which ones? As within the entire sample, stability is at its minimum with WTO threat perception and expectations of defense cooperation between the US and West Europe. Moreover, for defense cooperation, change is in the same direction in our combined subsample as in the entire sample. For WTO threat perception, we find less foreign policy or peace researchers and union members who fear change for the worse than before; 32.5% instead of an earlier 36.4%. So, one may argue that foreign policy or peace researchers and union members seem to move still further away from general elite pessimism on this item than before. While such an interpretation is compatible with the data, the data do not support it strongly either, because the percentage change corresponds to 3 persons only. Or, even among least stable items, even where two deviant groups are combined (because of similar views and in order to increase the number of cases), it is impossible to say anything definite or even plausible about feedback of information and corresponding attitude change.

Looking for suggestive, rather than definite, findings in the table above, one may note that foreign policy or peace researchers have been much more prone to changing their mind, on CSCE or the defense budget, than union members. While it is tempting to speculate about this, as well as about some other minor differences, we should repress it. By and large, total sample and both subsamples exhibit instability of views for similar items, in roughly similar orders of magnitude, and where seemingly interesting differences occur, they are due to a handful (or less) of cases.

Elite Opinion and Mass Opinion

Elite and mass opinion are interdependent. According to theoretical notions about two-step flow of communication and opinion leadership (Lazarsfeld et al. 1948, Katz and Lazarsfeld 1955), elites form mass opinion. However, within a pluralistic democracy, there are competing elites who would like to influence mass opinion and to receive mass support. The necessity to find mass support limits the decision-latitude of governing and would-be governing elites, alike. As mass support for particular elites is conditional and may be withdrawn, masses also command some influence over elites. In general, one may assume a greater elite decision-latitude in political domains where mass involvement and interest are low, as well as under conditions of elite consensus.

The latter point is obvious: elite consensus limits within-elite competition and elite attempts to find mass support for divergent view-points and thereby decreases incentives for broad political participation.[23] As noted above, German elites demonstrate a remarkable degree of unity and consensus in foreign policy and national security affairs. This should be a factor promoting elite decision-latitude vis-à-vis mass opinion. On the other hand, there are two groups within the elite where the dominant consensus is still widely shared and a majority position. But it is open to vigorous minority opposition. These two groups, i.e., trade unions and foreign policy or peace researchers, however, are fairly well-placed within the communication system and therefore command some substantial proselytizing potential. Moreover, where the defense budget and acceptance of superpower leadership is concerned, the media join foreign policy or peace researchers and unionists in their critical views. Whereas the degree of elite consensus widens decision-latitude for German elites in national security affairs, the placement of deviant and divided elites restricts it.

What about the other factor influencing elite decision-latitude, about mass interest and mass attitudes? Three quotations from a famous American survey researcher may introduce us to the subject: "Large portions of an electorate do not have meaningful beliefs, even on issues that have formed the basis for intense political controversy among elites for substantial periods of time (Converse 1964, p.245)". Or, "of any direct participation in this history of ideas and the behavior it shapes, the mass is remarkably innocent (Converse 1964, p.225)". If such an assessment should hold somewhere it must be foreign affairs: "The weakest issue areas for the mass public were those most remote from its daily concerns, including foreign policy . . . The strongest issue areas at the time were those likely to be seen as "doorstep" matters . . . (Converse 1975, p.85)".

Rosenau (1961, p.35) believes that between 75 and 90% of the mass public do not care for foreign policy at all — at least in quiet times. If similar percentages apply to Germany, elites have much leeway. When asked about their interests in politics, the percentage of West Germans saying "yes" has varied between 41 and 49 in the 1970s (Noelle-Neumann 1976, p.63), i.e., more than half of the population does not really care about politics. If one further differentiates according to degree of interest, or if one chooses a more demanding cutpoint, one may come down to as little as 7% who profess a strong interest in politics. When asked about primary political concerns for the FRG, economic problems were chosen by 85% in 1975 and by 74% in 1976, whereas merely 4% in both years mentioned either avoidance of war between East and West or European integration (Noelle-Neumann 1976, p.221). If West German voters limit the decision-latitude of elites, it is much more likely to concern domestic politics and particularly economic and welfare issues rather than foreign affairs or national security (Kaase 1970; Klingemann 1973; Klingemann and Taylor 1977).

The tendency to neglect national security items may even be found within some non-expert elites. Wildenmann's (1968b, 1971) elite survey is biased exactly in the opposite way from ours, i.e., his sample excludes the military and includes sub-national (state or "Länder") elites, whereas ours contains ca. 25% military and more than 50% who say that they are full-time and professionally concerned with national security and related matters. In Wildenmann's (1968b, p.156, 157) survey, consolidation of public finances, improvement of the educational system, and economic growth were chosen as definitely more important than better relationships with either superpower. Most of Wildenmann's elites lack expertise in national security and profess a rank ordering of concerns quite similar to the mass public. Mass public and non-expert elites are most likely to intrude into foreign and national security affairs, i.e., to limit expert decision-latitude where such policies become costly and therefore compete with domestic and more widely perceived, as well as understood, needs (compare Huntington 1975 for the American case).[24] Or, the defense budget may be the Archilles' heel of any national security policy, even if it commands overwhelming expert or elite support.

There is some evidence that elite opinions set the agenda for public discussion and policy; that elite attitudes predict what is going to happen. In 1968, elites overwhelmingly rejected a continuation of the grand (CDU/CSU + SPD) coalition after the 1969 election inspite of their feeling that such a grand coalition had been necessary. Moreover, educational reform, democratization, and better relations with the East and the USSR were highly ranked issues among elites (see Wildenmann 1971, p.57-59). One year later, in 1969, Brandt formed his Social Democratic-Liberal government which excluded Christian Democrats and responded to those issues. Governing Social Democratic and Liberal elites even changed public opinion by their policies. According to Klingemann (1973, p. 243) willingness to accord legal acknowledgement to the GDR rose from 31 to 61% between 1969 and 1972, i.e., after 3 years of Brandt's chancellorship. However, we should not make too much of elite capability to control events. While educational background is a poor substitute for belonging to an elite, we nevertheless want to remind readers that in 1946, less educated Americans foresaw the future development of US-USSR relations much more correctly than their better educated counterparts

(Hofstätter 1966, p. 156). In foreign affairs, elite hopes and expectations may easily be nullified by forces beyond national control.

Even within mass opinion there is an awareness that national security problems exist. When asked in October 1975, whether peace in Europe is still threatened from the East, or whether pacts ("Ostverträge") persistently secured peace, a majority of 48% either could not decide in favor of one alternative over the other one or simply said "don't know". Results show that 38% felt that peace is still threatened, while 14% chose the optimistic evaluation of "Ostpolitik" (Noelle-Neumann 1976, p.283).Given the difference in wording the questions in mass public surveys and in our elite survey, and given in fact that our elite sample is nothing better than accidental, it is difficult to evaluate those responses in comparison to elite opinion. Nevertheless, in our opinion, these data suggest that a 38:14 majority of articulate Germans feel threatened, i.e., a higher than 2/3 majority in the articulate public. Futher evidence comes from another mass survey (INFAS 1976, table 1.01A) where 61% attribute expansionism to the Soviet bloc. Being threatened creates the necessity for deterrence in the first place. Inspite of severe doubts the defensibility of West Germany — 11% think it is impossible, another 41% consider the prospects of successful defense as dubious (INFAS 1976, table 1.07A) — 62% want to resist a military attack (INFAS 1976, table 1.06A). The close-to-2-out-of-3 majority of those who feel threatened from the Soviet bloc and who want to resist, compares well with the ca. 70% of our elite respondents who attribute peace between East and West to deterrence. Without claiming more than plausibility for our interpretation, we perceive a fair degree of similarity between elite and mass opinion an threat perception and deterrence.

When asked in 1976 a series of questions about NATO, 46% said that NATO preserved peace for the Western World, 35% said without NATO we (West Germany) would already belong to the Soviet bloc, and still 28% believed that the Soviets fear NATO defenses (Noelle-Neumann 1976, p.291). Again, it is difficult to evaluate those numbers, in particular because respondents were not asked to respond to each item separately. While the 46% in the general public sample fall below the 70% who subscribed to deterrence in our elite sample, this difference does not necessarily indicate more skepticism about NATO and deterrence in the general public. First, different types of questions do elicit different answers. Second, our accidental elite sample may deviate from general opinion, not because it is elite, but rather because it is accidental. Third, such questions are obviously less meaningful to the general public than to elites and therefore, the 54% not attributing peace to NATO may consist more of "don't knows" rather than of critics. With all these qualifications in mind, we still do not find evidence for any major difference between elite and mass opinion.

When asked about close cooperation with other nations, West Germans consistently choose the US more often than any other nation. In the 1970s, the percentage in favor of the US connection generally has been close to 80, whereas it has been 15% lower for France (Noelle-Neumann 1976, p.279). Although this question has not addressed itself to national security affairs in particular as did our elite questions, there is again some degree of similarity. Elites and mass public overwhelmingly prefer the US connection over any other policy alternative, if such alternatives were to exist.

However, there is one major item where elites and masses possibly differ. When asked about the best foreign policy (whether it is a military alliance with the US or Swiss-type neutrality), 51% preferred the US connection, and 38% Swiss-type neutrality (Noelle-Neumann 1976, p.279). While there definitely is a majority in favor of defense collaboration with the US, an important minority looks for a different solution. While elites — at least in our sample — consistently over a variety of questions and overwhelmingly support continuing status quo policies of deterrence and US connection, the general public seems somewhat less convinced. In over-time comparison, there does not seem to be much of a trend. If any trend exists, it seems to run in favor of the US connection and against neutralism (Noelle-Neumann 1974, p.535 and 1976, p.279).

Above we find that West German elites are gloomy and pessimistic: they do not expect their hopes to be fulfilled. Instead, they are afraid of changes for the worse. Similar pessimism can be found in West German mass opinion. In 1975, 37% expected the USSR to become more powerful 50 years later, while merely 13% expected the US still then to top the USSR (Noelle-Neumann 1976, p.280). Even a combination of the percentages of those who expect either the US to stay strongest or both superpowers to be equally strong in 50 years, yields only 35%, still less than the 37% who see rising Soviet power. Pessimism about the changing balance of power is matched by pessimism about NATO's capability to defend West Germany. In March 1976, 26% believed there are enough troops, 28% thought we (and NATO) could not defend ourselves (Noelle-Neumann 1976, p.291). In another survey (INFAS 1976, table 1.07A), figures turned out somewhat different but about as pessimistic: 11% think it is impossible to defend West Germany, while another 41% judge the prospect as dubious.

The issues of neutralism notwithstanding, by and large, mass opinion is pretty much in accord with elite opinion on the two basic topics of national security; on deterrence and the desirability of maintaining close cooperation with the United States. The differences which exist seem to be typical of elite-mass differences in general. Elites seem more articulate and coherent in their views. This should hardly come as much of a surprise.

Summary and Conclusion

First of all, we want to remind our readers of some caveats. It is extremely difficult to tell who belongs to an elite. We do not even believe in a dichotomous conceptualization of elite. We suspect that "eliteness" is more fruitfully conceptualized as a continuum, rather than as a dichotomy where one either belongs to an elite or does not belong. If our suspicion has some merit to it, then any cutpoint is essentially arbitrary. Or, even a description of the West German elite "universe" is fruitless. Under such circumstances random sampling is impossible and representativeness is hard to achieve. Thus, our sample is nothing better than accidental. Textbook rules of social research teach us that results from accidental samples may be as accidental as the sample itself. While we do not want to contend with rigorous and basically well-founded methodological views, we feel that our enterprise is justified by the fact that nothing better than what we have done is currently available, or even feasible. Some information, however limited its value, may be preferable to none at all.

In a certain respect, however, our sample has been selected in such a way as to systematically differ from a "representative" (if that were at all possible) elite sample. We consciously focused on elites who are professionally concerned with national security and related foreign policy issues. The 56% who claimed professional concern with such matters may serve as an indication of our degree of success. But the very success of getting hold of a sample where professional concern with national security is extremely high also may be viewed as a source of distortion. National security elites may systematically differ in their views on national security from other elites, and the latter's views still might be important even on national security issues. As reported above, military experience and other military background variables have some impact. Typically, Realist as well as Atlanticist orientations are reinforced by military background. As our sample is biased in favor of including those who, like the military, are professionally concerned with national security,[25] we may have given undue weight to a particular elite sector and its views. In part, this may account for the extremely high degree of consensus we found among our respondents. However, one should not make too much of this. Even among those groups who are most deviant in their views, i.e., among unions, foreign policy or peace researchers, and the young, the generally accepted views dominate, although less overwhelmingly than elsewhere. While sample bias due to oversampling expert elites rather than potential counter-elites may have somewhat exaggerated the degree of consensus among West German elites, we find little reason to suspect a fundamentally altered picture to result from any other reasonable sampling or weighting scheme. Although such problems undoubtedly exist in our survey, the extraordinary degree of consensus found across groupings and categories reassures us that any bias in favor of some elite groups or sectors, at the expense of others, has fairly limited effects.

In an overall summary, an overwhelming majority of respondents provides "Realist" replies to national security questions. The German elite consents that deterrence reduces the risk of war and attributes peace between East and West to deterrence. It is ready to pay a price for deterrence by acceptance of superpower leadership and bipolarity. It rejects criticism of Western defense efforts as unfounded and even accepts the necessity of higher German defense expenditures. By contrast, German elites are fairly skeptical about détente-related policies. The usefulness of CSCE is much more in doubt than is the usefulness of deterrence. More respondents are afraid of the West falling behind in the arms race than of the risks of war inherent in arms races. There is strong opposition against unbalanced reductions of armed forces in Central Europe. Few, indeed, believe in an atmosphere of détente as a substitute to deterrence. And there is little hope that economic cooperation and trade across the Iron Curtain affect national security for the better. While there is a sizeable minority who desires a more active foreign policy for the FRG, there is little consensus among this minority on any specific actions to be taken. And, the minority divided among itself is faced by a solid majoritiy.

German elites desire European as well as Atlantic cooperation. While majorities favor cooperation across various domains — like military affairs, foreign policy, economics, or even social welfare policy — as well as across contexts, whether European or Atlantic, consensus is maximized where defense cooperation with the United States is concerned. While German elites are worried and concerned about expectations of not getting what they want from the Western alliance, trust in the US commitment to military cooperation with Western Europe is better than trust in the reliability or workability of purely "European" solutions to security problems. Our respondents are, nevertheless, worried about US troop withdrawals. While hopes and expectations for defense matters center around the US, in economic affairs there is less of a US-orientation to be found. Whereas German elites predict that Western cooperation in national security affairs falls short of desirable levels, they simultaneously predict future Soviet successes in the military integration of Eastern Europe.

In the sixties, an American scholar (Hanrieder 1967, p.1) wrote: "The absence of viable alternatives is often regarded as the outstanding characteristic of West German foreign policy. There is much truth in this assessment." We could not agree more to such a statement as an adequate description of the present state of affairs, even one decade later. While exact comparisons between our study and earlier research are impossible, it nevertheless has to be pointed out, that Deutsch et al. (1967) found in their 1964 survey a similar focus of West German security thinking on the US and a similar excess of trust in the US as compared to trust in fellow Europeans, as we did. On this highly important topic, there is little evidence for change between 1964 and 1976.

If German elites do not perceive meaningful alternatives to present and status quo-oriented policies, this does not mean that overwhelming support for such policies is given lightheartedly. Quite to the contrary. Our elite is a worried and pessimistic elite. While few hope for détente-related policies to overcome the necessity for deterrence or even to support and supplement it meaningfully and significantly, our elite is well aware of the inherent limitations of deterrence as a device for ensuring long-run survival. Whereas they feel that improved relations between East and West should be accompanied by better cooperation within the West, expectations concerning East-West and intra-Western cooperation are not equally strongly correlated. Whereas respondents expect some correspondence between Soviet goals and likely achievements in fastening their grip on Eastern Europe, they expect Western integration to fall short of the desirable. Whereas German elites do not see any workable alternatives to continuing present policies, they nevertheless do not expect any positive developments to derive therefrom. Instead, the outlook is gloomy. Where pockets of optimism exist, as in economic matters, such optimism is contained with no carry-over to security-related issues.[26]

What is behind that gloomy consensus? In our opinion, German elite views are in response to the strategic location of West Germany and problems resulting therefrom. The security dilemma, both between the superpowers and between their respective alliances, still exists. Moreover, West Germany is a front state located in an exposed and vulnerable forward position as it is. In addition, Germany is a divided nation. Therefore, both German states find it extremely difficult to accord legitimacy to each other. In addition to these problems there is West Berlin and the continuing ideological and value conflict between East and West. Therefore, continuing and severe conflicts of interest between East and West, focused on and in Germany, may be taken for granted. Germans know that if deterrence should fail, if war in Europe breaks out, we are the first casualties. Tactical nuclear warfare in Central Europe might result from Soviet conventional superiority and result in something close to extermination of Germany's population (Weizsäcker 1971). The magnitude of the threat combined with extremely limited German potential to influence, not to speak of control, the course of events should go far in explaining threat perception as well as reliance on the only power in the world that can provide counterbalancing power and protection against Soviet pressures. In our interpretation, existing conflicts of interest – both worldwide and Central European — account for the broadly based consensus on having no choice other than deterrence which is feasible only in cooperation with the US. While this interpretation is not testable with our data, at least it is testable in principle. If it should be true, similar views on deterrence as well as on cooperation with the United States should prevail among elites in nations which are located close to or within zones of conflict such as Turkey, Israel, or South Korea, while elites in societies who have the good luck of living in quiet, privileged, and peaceful corners of the world, e.g., Scandinavia, should be more skeptical of deterrence as well as less pro-US, and simultaneously place much more faith in good will and détente to overcome conflicts of interest. The propositions that concern about deterrence is a function of perceived conflicts of interest, and that reliance on the United States is a function of facing a Communist threat, may be embedded in a wider theoretical framework which links objective realities of world politics with perceptions, and finally, with actual conflict behavior among nations. Within such a framework (Weede 1975a, 1975b, 1976, 1977a), the same set of background variables serves to account for elite views, military preparedness, and actual conflict behavior.

Some indirect evidence in support of a geostrategic or ecological approach in the explanation of national security views may be derived from the 1964 survey of French as well as German elites (Deutsch 1967, Deutsch et al. 1967): There was a stronger Atlantic orientation in West Germany than in France, a stronger feeling of strategic dependence on the US in West Germany than in France, much more belief in the workability of an independent deterrent and defense stance in France than in West Germany, and a much more positive attitude towards bipolarity in West Germany than in France. Why? As West Germany, in contrast to France, borders the Iron Curtain (which is more, rather than less, of an Iron Curtain in 1978 compared to Stalin's days when East Germans could travel and escape to the West easier than they can today) and directly faces Soviet tanks and divisions, we are more dependent on the US, and therefore are more favorably disposed toward Atlantic cooperation and cannot entertain the belief of being able to resist Soviet pressure on our own. We therefore do not expect improvements from mulitpolarity. Even in a multipolar world, the USSR will stay as, or nearly as, close to West Germany as it is today. But multipolarity might imply less countervailing American power to balance Soviet capabilities. (If West Germany should ever be overrun by Soviet troops, we confidently predict "West German" attitudes among the French elite as a result).

Though comparability of our survey and elite surveys covering other nations is extremely low, because other surveys differ from ours in items asked in the questionnaire, in sample size, composition, and even in the time when the survey was undertaken, we nevertheless find some comparisons interesting and suggestive. According to Hart's (1976) survey of 73 Swedish security elite members in winter 72/73, Swedish elites seem to demonstrate a comparable degree of consensus on some basic issues as West German elites do, i.e., they agree with each other on the desirability of armed neutrality and freedom from alliances about as strongly as West Germans do on deterrence and the need to maintain the US connection. As in the West German case, some scientists deviate somewhat from general elite opinion. However, Swedish security elites are much more optimistic than are German elites. In our opinion, this is what one should expect if geostrategic realities and involvement in related conflicts of interest are used to deduce elite views.

Similarly, the Russett and Hanson (1975) surveys of 567 leading businessmen and 621 military elite members, both conducted early in 1973, demonstrate much more American optimism about the Communist threat than is the case in West Germany. Whereas 57.8% of US business and still 39.6% of the US military perceived a decreased threat (Russett and Hanson 1975, p. 273), merely 8.7% of our West German elite expressed similar optimism in a somewhat similar question. While different questions, and probably more importantly, different times, are likely to explain some of the difference observed, the results are also compatible with the view that the objectively greater vulnerability of West Germany compared to the US, as well as the smaller degree of national control, in the West German case, lead to more pessimistic attitudes. Finally, there is another interesting difference between American and West German data. Whereas 69% of our West German elites saw no impact of economic cooperation between East and West on military security, and only slightly more Germans (18.9%) could imagine a positive rather than a negative (12.0%)impact, 61.5% of US business and 44.1% of the US military consider "trade, technical cooperation, and economic interdependence" to constitute the "most important approach to world peace" (Russett and Hanson 1975, p. 271). Again, questions and time of questioning differ. Nevertheless, there still seems to remain a true difference in hopes attached to a "peace by trade" strategy. Deep involvement in severe conflicts of interest, combined with little or no national capability to independently defend one's homeland, are objective background factors which have to be taken into consideration when West German elite views and elite pessimism are evaluated.

Of course, our interpretation of German elite consensus is not at all unique. In the late sixties, Hanrieder (1967, p. 5) offered a fairly similar interpretation: "There is considerable evidence that the restrictions and opportunities of the international operational environment provided the West German government with a relatively narrow range of acceptable alternatives". In some places, Hanrieder (1967, p. 93, 198) even seems to imply that it is the very absence of acceptable and feasible alternatives that explains German consensus on national security and foreign policy issues. So far, his analysis concurs with and supplements ours. Moreover, we find it convenient to apply his concept of a penetrated political system to West Germany. According to Hanrieder (1967, p. 230), "a political system is penetrated (1) if its decision-making process regarding the allocation of values or the mobilization of support on behalf of its goals is strongly affected by external events, and (2) if it can command wide consensus among the relevant elements of the decision-making process in accommodating to these elements". Hanrieder's first criterion undoubtedly applies to Germany, but it might apply to many other states, possibly including even the superpowers. However, a nation is penetrated only if the second criterion is also fulfilled; if the response to external events is "accommodating" and can command "wide consensus". The latter condition exists according to our results. Moreover, the consensus is accommodating, because nearly two thirds of our respondents are ready to accept superpower — i.e., American — guidance for the sake of peace. Similarly, Deutsch et al. (1964, p. 181 and 266) found a "sense of dependence on the United States" as well as some "emotional ties to the bipolar perspective" among their respondents in 1964. Further evidence comes from Schatz and his study of the German Bundestag and its defense committee. In 1964, less than 10% of his respondents could imagine that West Europe, even if united, could ever face the USSR on its own (Schatz 1970, p. 212). Moreover, Bundestag members even attributed as high, or higher, influence on the West German defense budget either to the US or NATO, if compared to either FRG government or FRG legislative influence. We Germans are penetrated, we have known it for a long time and we perceive no workable alternative.

Historically, of course, West Germany was foundet as a penetrated political system. Before 1955, West Germany even met Rosenau's (1966, p. 65) more stringent criteria for penetration: "A penetrated political system is one in which nonmembers of a national society participate directly and authoritatively, through actions taken jointly with the society's members, in either the allocation of its values or the mobilization of support on behalf of its goals". Similarly, German observers, like Wildenmann (1967), point out that West German policy-making, in those days, required a consensus of Western allies and of Germans, and of victors and vanquished. In the late forties and early fifties, West Germany was penetrated according to Rosenau's criteria. She also had not yet achieved a broad-based consensus on foreign policy and national security. In those days, West Germany was a burden, rather than an asset, to the Western Alliance. While German rearmament was begun in 1955, it became finally accepted by all politically relevant forces in 1960, when the Social Democrats grudgingly accepted the basic tenets of Adenauer's foreign policy. Since then, electoral results or changes of government can no longer be imagined to affect the basic principles of West German foreign policy. Or, no imaginable electoral result can destabilize Germany's willing and effective participation in the defense of Western Europe.

Which processes or events did produce this change of mind on part of the Social Democrats? First, there is little reason to attribute the Social Democratic reversal on national security to public opinion and its pressure (see Hütter, 1975, and the mass survey evidence quoted therein). Quite to the contrary, mass surveys revealed that Social Democrats came closer to majority opinion than did Christian Democrats. Why did they nevertheless change their minds? While it has been suggested (Hütter 1975, p. 155) that Social Democrats may have reversed their position in order to become elegible for junior partner in a grand coalition with the Christian Democrats, we believe this explanation does not tell the major part of the story.

Why did Social Democrats lose election after election in spite of being closer to public opinion with regard to national security in the fifties? Assuming that there is something to Hütter's argument, why did they have to look forward to sneaking into the government via the backdoor rather than triumphantly entering the frontdoor after electoral victory? For the first part of the argument, we may follow Hanrieder's (1967, p. 78) or Wildenmann's (1967, p. 15–18) guidance. In the fifties, there was a certain contradiction between rearmament and Western integration to deter Soviet threats, on the one hand, and German reunification, on the other hand. Adenauer and the Christian Democratic governments defined a concept of national security that focused on West Germany and its ties with the Western world but which effectively postponed or downgraded the priority given to immediate and possibly risky reunification (Besson 1968, Hanrieder 1967, Hütter 1975, Wildenmann 1967). By itself, this policy choice might have spelled grave risks for the Christian Democrats. However, Adenauer's Western policy "not only was compatible with the goal of political recovery but was its prerequisite" (Hanrieder 1967, p. 83). If the world political situation in those days put a premium on a narrow, i.e., *West* German rather than German definition of national security, or if a Western policy only carried economic benefits with it, then Adenauer and his Christian Democrats could afford to lose a few voters because of their foreign policy as long as they could hope for electoral benefits coming from economic recovery. As is well known, German voters, like voters in other nations, give more weight to economic success than to foreign policy issues (Kaase 1970; Noelle-Neumann 1976, p. 221; Klingemann 1973; Klingemann and Taylor 1977). You cannot beat the boom and some politicians may know or feel it.

If it is the association with economic benefits that invigorated political support for Adenauer, the Christian Democrats, and their defense policies, then the Social Democrats did not have to reverse themselves because their arguments failed within the field of military security and foreign policy, but because either they did not understand the linkage between a strictly *West* German definition of national security and prospects for economic recovery in the fifties, or they did not understand the impact of economic success on voting behavior. The security-recovery linkage ruling out unification by neutralization plus US-supported recovery was a given, not of Germany's choosing, but all the more powerful for that matter.

As we pointed out above, even in the mid- and late seventies, support for the foreign and national security policy inherited from Adenauer is still stronger among Christian Democrats than among Social Democrats, trade unions (who are traditionally close to the Social Democrats),Liberals. However, these vestiges of contemporary history do not endanger German elite consensus. Even among these more divided elites, consensus on most basic issues is still solid. While they demand something like CSCE, in addition to traditional deterrence and Western orientation, they do not want to replace it. Within the elite, consensus seems firm and unshakeable. While we find it hard to imagine any internally-conditioned breakup of the consensus on national security[27] and on deterrence in close cooperation with the US, it is easier to think of scenarios where external events enforce a reorientation. An obvious, though hopefully unlikely, illustration is an American decision to withdraw from Continental Europe. If the protector of a dependent nation ceases to be protector, then the dependent nation faces an entirely different situation. A less extreme, and therefore somewhat more likely, scenario might refer to the gradual erosion of credibility of American guarantees due to ever-improving Soviet nuclear capablilities. Finally, domestic events in other West European societies might put Germany in a situation where equally close collaboration with European neighbors and the US could become more and more difficult (see Dahrendorf 1976). Let us underline our view that international or world political processes are more likely to force a major foreign policy change in West Germany than any conceivable outcomes of power-contests between elite factions: US foreign policy might be the most important single factor that influences where German foreign policy will move. German elites do not seem to imagine anything better than the status quo, inspite of their insight in the inherent limitations of the status quo, inspite of their doubts whether a deterioration can be avoided. The status quo depends on US commitment.

Notes

1 Somewhat to our surprise, we found overwhelming consensus on most basic items, and within most of our subsamples. At least in Weede's opinion the consensus found makes Delphi rather meaningless on most points. While we do report some results from the second wave below, they merely reinforce conclusions based on first wave results. By and large, Delphi-related features of the SIPLA project are controversial among the authors of this book.

2 When doing an elite study of his own, even a former student of Dahrendorf (Zapf 1965, p. 73, 76) had to admit the arbitrariness of any cutpoints separating elite from non-elite persons.

3 For practical reasons, it was impossible to make all elite members respond at the very same time or within a shorter period of time. In our view, there have been no events within the first half of 1976 which deeply affected West German elite opinion — not even the fall of Angola. As channel of access is confounded with response time, we do not think it is meaningful to compare responses over months or weeks when questionnaires were returned. Moreover, return date and actual response date may differ. The latter one is more important, but unknown. Furthermore, the consensus, to be reported below, makes it rather unlikely that time of response had a major impact on results.

4 In Weede's opinion such a judgement presupposes a systematic comparison of causal assertions made by elites and relevant quantitative evidence. Some first and tentative steps in that direction have been undertaken by Rummel (1976); Weede (1977b); Weede and Schössler (1978).

5 Wildenmann (1968, p. 2; 1971, p. 50) and Schleth (1971, p. 113) report 57% Protestants, 26% Catholics, and 15% without religious identification. For a different and larger sample, Hoffmann-Lange (1976, p. 34) reports 56.5% Protestants, 30.3% Catholics, and 12.4% without religious identification. Zapf's (1965, p. 174, 175) study of German elites demonstrates that Catholics have been fairly successful in entering the political elite (parties, governments) after WW II and up to 1955, but much less so in the military, business or administration.

6 In our opinion, there is still no practicable substitute to a multivariate analysis of ordinal variables which treats ordinal variables as if they were interval (Kim 1975). Therein, we find some comfort from the results of Labovitz (1970). Because of Doreian's (1972) work we did not reduce the number of categories in our original scales before doing the factor analysis.

7 Heavily skewed distributions also may imply severe problems of robustness if one has nothing better than rank order categories as we do (Abelson and Tukey 1970).

8 Within psychology, this is known as the problem of difficulty factors. Although it is discussed for dichotomous variables only (e.g., Rummel 1970, p. 304), it may always arise where distributional asymmetries restrict ranges of correlation coefficients, as they do here in our data set.
While Pearson's correlation coefficient is required for factor analysis, whereas gamma is somewhat illegitimate for that purpose, we did a factor analysis based on both kinds of input. Fortunately, we found fairly similar results. For bivariate applications, however, we prefer gamma in order to overcome correlation sensitivity to marginal distributions and their asymmetries.

9 Gamma-based hierarchical clustering (as in OSIRIS 3) produced results most similar to those of a product-moment-correlation-based factor analysis. Both, gamma-based factor

analysis and gamma-based hierarchical clustering tend to propose a split-up of the "Realism-Idealism"- or "Deterrence-Détente"-grouping. In our opinion, however, to do so makes little sense from a substantive point of view. Results from multidimensional scaling (as in OSIRIS 3) are least interpretable and most dissimilar to all other results.

10 According to Russett and Hanson (1975, p. 271), American business and military elites demonstrate much more readiness to subscribe to "peace by trade"-views. Or, at least they did in 1973, when 61.5% of business and 44.1% of military elites considered "trade, technical cooperation, and economic interdependence" as "the most important approach to world peace". For quantitative evidence against such hopes, see Russett 1967; Rummel 1966, 1972, 1976; von Atta and Robertson 1976.

11 As in our previous analyses and comparisons, product-moment-correlation-based factor analysis, gamma-based factor analysis, and hierarchical clustering (as in OSIRIS 3) produce fairly similar solutions, whereas results from multidimensional scaling (as in OSIRIS 3) are hardly interpretable.

12 While being foreign minister of the FRG, Brandt (1967) published an article, where he stressed the necessity to base détente on a secure basis of Western cooperation. After 1969, it has always been a bone of contention between Brandt's government and opposition Christian Democrats whether détente, on the one hand, and deterrence and Western cooperation, on the other hand, are indeed compatible (e.g., Haftendorn 1975, p. 342; or Schwarz 1972). For American adherents of the (partial) incompatibility hypothesis, see Holsti, Hopmann, Sullivan (1973, p. 145).

13 Party membership as understood in this chapter refers to professed membership, not to channel of access. For example, only 122 respondents have been accessed via Social Democratic Party (SPD) channels. Nevertheless, 226 said they were Social Democrats. The difference between channel of access and membership is even more important among Christian Democrats. Here, approximately half of them have been reached via official party channels.

14 For 1964, Schatz (1970, p. 143) reports more unity and consensus among Social Democrats rather than among Christian Democrats. The difference between his and our findings may be due to either change or the higher level of abstractness and hypothetical content in our study as compared to Schatz's.

15 In the 1964 study by Schatz (1970, p. 212), Liberals differed from others by being more optimistic about the capability of a United West Europe to stand alone vis-à-vis the Soviet Union. If they should still hold this optimistic view (what we cannot know), reluctance to accept superpower leadership would be understandable. The attitude toward defense expenditure would not be. Of course, we cannot rule out the possibility that Liberal deviancy in the earlier study as well as in ours is an artifact due to small numbers.

16 All of the military background variables refer to self-report in the questionnaire and not to channel of access. Whether we contacted a military officer via military command lines, or somehow differently, does not matter.

17 Whereas West German military and civilian elites hardly differ in their views on the defense budget, Russett and Hanson (1975, p. 277) report major differences between business and military elites in the US in 1973. There, 42.7% of the military, but only 19.9% of business, advocated a rising defense budget.

18 Being a foreign policy or peace researcher is operationalized by channel of access and not by self-report. In practice, it means employment by research institutions or universities.

19 Trade union membership means professed union membership in the questionnaire. The

number of union members is much higher than the number of those who have been accessed via union channels.

20 Employment in the media is inferred from channel of access and does not refer to any item in the questionnaire.

21 For the US in 1973, Lefever (1976) provides some extremely interesting data which demonstrate how little information about basic national security problems even the prestige media may carry, while simultaneously delegitimizing both the government and its national security efforts.

22 The term responsibility is used in a strictly formal sense. No moral connotations are implied. However, we do feel that foreign policy or peace research institutions have fairly little influence on political decision making. As answers to the professional concern item demonstrate, foreign policy and peace researchers share such an assessment.

23 Similar points are made elsewhere. According to Nie and Verba (1975, p. 55), "social conflict, particularly when structured by political parties, enhances equality" and mass participation. — Huntington and Nelsón (1976, p. 29) argue that political elites out of power try to expand political participation in order to create a power base of their own. If there is much elite consensus, then there is less incentive to take issues to the mass public and voters.

24 According to Wildenmann (1967, 1968a), there is some tension or even contradiction between national mobilization of political support or national consensus-building, on the one hand, and the international linkages and organizations within the West, on the other hand. Such a state of affairs not only endangers democratic control of foreign and national security policy, but also may be a factor reinforcing parochial and provincial attitudes toward national security. Such a lack of familiarity and understanding may result in resistance to more vigorous Western defense efforts that may become essential some day.

25 Active military duty and professional concern with national security are highly correlated: gamma is 0.96 and even phi is 0.49. Nearly half of those who claim professional concern are active soldiers. And nearly all (97%) active soldiers claim concern. Saying that one is concerned is correlated with belief in deterrence (gamma is 0.19 or 0.23 depending on the question asked), with a strong desire for close and continuous defense cooperation with the United States (gamma is 0.26) and with support for higher defense spending (gamma is 0.16). However, professed concern is unrelated to détente items like CSCE support, hopes in peace by trade, or the belief that an atmosphere of détente promotes peace. Professed concern, also, is independent of the proposed role for the FRG and readiness to accept superpower leadership. By and large, professional concern means still less deviation from generally held views.

26 Possibly, there is some transfer of pessimism from national security to other political domains. Dahrendorf (1965, p. 297 ff.) describes the West German elites as a cartel of anxiety and deplores the resulting political stagnation. Refering to the 1950s, Deutsch and Edinger (1959, p. 47) observe: "some of the determinants of German foreign policy were likely to be negative: to avoid or delay any decisions that might make matters worse«. Thus, anxiety and pessimism about the future seem to be widely accepted traits of West German (foreign policy) elites.

27 Deutsch and Edinger (1959, p. 193) argue that "German political consensus and stability appear markedly vulnerable to changes at home or abroad". In 1964, Deutsch, Edinger, Macridis and Merritt (1967, p. 133) collected elite opinions on Germany's likely reaction to crisis. About half of their respondents were confident and the other half either anxious or uncertain. Even in the early seventies, Wildenmann (1971, p. 19, 20) expressed his

doubts about democratic stability, because the '66-'67 recession gave rise to a rigth wing party (NPD) and because of lack of "affective relations to democracy". After West Germany has had about 1 million unemployed for more than a year without a radical protest vote or other threats to democratic stability, we feel that a more optimistic attitude towards the West German system and its domestic crisis stability is warranted.

References

ABELSON, R. P. and J. W. TUKEY (1970) "Efficient Conversion of Non-Metric into Metric Information", pp. 407–417, in E.R. Tufte (ed.): *The Quantitative Analysis of Social Problems.* Reading, Mass: Addison-Wesley.

AUTON, G.P. (1976) "Nuclear Deterrence and the Medium Power: A Proposal for Doctrinal Change in the British and French Cases". *Orbis* 20: 367–400.

AXELROD, R. (1976) *Structure of Decision.* Princeton University Press.

BESSON, W. (1968) " Prinzipienfragen der westdeutschen Außenpolitik". *Politische Vierteljahresschrift* 9: 28–44.

BRANDT. W. (1967) "Entspannungspolitik mit langem Atem". *Außenpolitik* 18, Heft 8: 449–454.

BURNS, A.L. (1968) *Of Powers and Their Politics: A Critique of Theoretical Approaches.* Englewood Cliffs, N.J.: Prentice-Hall.

CAMPBELL, D.T. and T.H. McCORMACK (1957) "Military Experience and Attitudes toward Authority". *American Journal of Sociology* 62, 1957, 482–490.

CONVERSE, P.E. (1964) "The Nature of Belief Systems in Mass Publics". D.E. Apter (ed.): *Ideology and Discontent.* New York: Free Press.

CONVERSE, P.E. (1975) "Public Opinion and Voting Behavior", pp. 75–169, in F.I. Greenstein and N.W. Polsby (eds.): *Handbook of Political Science.* Volume 4: Nongovernmental Politics. Reading, Mass.: Addison-Wesley.

DAHRENDORF, R. (1961) *Gesellschaft und Freiheit.* München: Piper.

DAHRENDORF, R. (1965) *Gesellschaft und Demokratie in Deutschland.* München: Piper.

DAHRENDORF, R. (1976) "Themen, die keiner nennt". *Die Zeit* 39:6 und *Die Zeit* 40:9–10.

DEUTSCH, K.W. and L.J. EDINGER (1959) *Germany Rejoins the Power.* Stanford: Stanford University Press.

DEUTSCH, K.W. (1967) *Arms Control and the Altlantic Alliance.* New York: Wiley.

DEUTSCH, K.W., L.J. EDINGER, R.C. MACRIDIS, R.L. MERRITT (1967) *France, Germany, and the Western Alliance.* New York: Scribner's Sons.

DOREIAN, P. (1972) "Mulitvariate Analysis and Categorized Data" *Quality and Quantity* 6:253–272

ENKE, E., P. SCHMIDT, D. SCHÖSSLER (1976) "Sicherheitspolitische Planungsprobleme der Bundesrepublik Deutschland". *DGFK–Informationen* 2/76:17–20.

ENKE, E. und D. SCHÖSSLER (1977) "Sicherheitspolitische Handlungspotentiale in der Bundesrepublik Deutschland – am Beispiel von Experteneinstellungen zur KSZE", pp. 217–225 in J. Delbrück, N. Ropers, G. Zellentin (eds.): *Grünbuch zu den Folgewirkungen der KSZE.* Köln: Verlag Wissenschaft und Politik.

FLECKENSTEIN, B. und D. SCHÖSSLER (1973) "Jugend und Streitkräfte: Einstellungen der jungen Generation in der BRD". *Beiträge zur Konfliktforschung* 3, Heft 2, 1973, 29–72.

HAFTENDORN, H. (1974) *Abrüstungs- und Entspannungspolitik zwischen Sicherheitsbefriedigung und Friedenssicherung: Zur Außenpolitik der BRD 1955–1973.* Düsseldorf: Bertelsmann Universitätsverlag.

HANRIEDER, W.F. (1967) *West German Foreign Policy 1949–1963: International Pressure and Domestic Response.* Stanford: Stanford University Press.

HART, T.G. (1976) *The Cognitive World of Swedish Security Elites.* Stockholm: Scandinavian University Books.

HOFFMANN-LANGE, U. (1976) *Politische Einstellungsmuster in der Westdeutschen Führungsschicht.* Dissertation, Universität Mannheim.

HOFSTÄTTER, P.R. (1966) *Einführung in die Sozialpsychologie.* Stuttgart: Kröner.

HOLSTI, O.R., P.T. HOPMANN, J.D. SULLIVAN (1973) *Unity and Disintegration in International Alliances.* New York: Wiley.

HUNTINGTON, S.P. (1975) "The United States", pp. 59–118 in M. Crozier, S.P. Huntington, J. Watanuki (eds.): *The Crisis of Democracy.* New York: New York University Press.

HUNTINGTON, S.P. and J.M. NELSON (1976) *No Easy Choice: Political Participation in Developing Countries.* Cambridge: Harvard University Press.

HÜTTER, J. (1975) *SPD und nationale Sicherheit.* Meisenheim am Glan: Hain.

INFAS (1976) *Verteidigungsklima 1976.* Tabellenband. Bonn: Institut für Angewandte Sozialwissenschaft.

JENNINGS, M.K. and G.B. MARKUS (1977) "The Effect of Military Service on Political Attitudes: A Panel Study". *American Political Science Review* LXXI, 1977, 131–147.

KAASE, M. (1970) "Determinanten des Wahlverhaltens bei der Bundestagswahl 1969". *Politische Vierteljahresschrift* 11:46–110.

KATZ, E. and P.F. LAZARSFELD (1955) *Personal Influence.* Glencoe, Ill.: Free Press.

KIM, J.-O. (1975) "Multivariate Analysis of Ordinal Variables". *American Journal of Sociology* 81:261–298.

KLINGEMANN, H.D. (1973) "Issue-Kompetenz und Wahlentscheidung". *Politische Vierteljahresschrift* 14:227–256.

KLINGEMANN, H.D. und CH.L. TAYLOR (1977) "Affektive Parteiorientierung, Kanzlerkandidaten und Issues. Einstellungskomponenten der Wahlentscheidung bei Bundestagswahlen in Deutschland". *Politische Vierteljahresschrift* 18, 1977, 301–347.

LABOVITZ, S. (1970) "The Assignment of Numbers to Rank Order Categories". *American Sociological Review* 35:515–524.

LAZARSFELD, P., B. BERELSON, and H. GAUDET (1948) *The People's Choice.* New York: Columbia University Press.

LEFEVER, E.W. (1976) "The Prestige Press, Foreign Policy, and American Survival". *Orbis* 20:207–226.

LINSTONE, H.A. and M. TUROFF (1975) *The Delphi Method: Techniques and Applications.* Reading, Mass: Addison-Wesley.

NIE, N.H. and S. VERBA (1975) "Political Participation", pp. 1–74 in F.I. Greenstein and N.W. Polsby (eds.): *Handbook of Political Science.* Volume 4: Nongovernmental Politics. Reading, Mass.: Addison-Wesley.

NOELLE, E. und E.P. NEUMANN (1974) *Jahrbuch der öffentlichen Meinung, 1968–1973.* Allensbach und Bonn: Verlag für Demoskopie.

NOELLE-NEUMANN, E. (1976) *Allensbacher Jahrbuch der Demoskopie 1974 – 1976* Band VI. Wien und München: Molden.

ROGHMANN, K. and W. SODEUR (1972) "The Impact of Military Service on Authoritarian Attitudes: Evidence from West Germany." *American Journal of Sociology* 78, 1972, 418–433.

ROSECRANCE, R. (1975) *Strategic Deterrence Reconsidered.* Adelphi Paper 116. London: International Institute for Strategic Studies.

ROSENAU, J.N. (1961) *Public Opinion and Foreign Policy.* New York: Random House.

ROSENAU, J.N. (1966) "Pre-theories and Theories of Foreign Policy", pp. 27–92 in R.B. Farrel (ed.): *Approaches to Comparative and International Politics.* Evanston, Ill.: Northwestern University Press.

RUMMEL, R.J. (1966) "Some Dimensions in the Foreign Behavior of Nations". *Journal of Peace Research* 3:201–224.

RUMMEL, R.J. (1970) *Applied Factor Analysis.* Evanston, Ill.: Northwestern University Press.

RUMMEL, R.J. (1972) *The Dimensions of Nations.* Beverly Hills, Calif.: Sage.

RUMMEL, R.J. (1976) *Peace Endangered.* Beverly Hills: Sage.

RUSSETT, B.M. (1967) *International Regions and the International System.* Chicago: Rand McNally.

RUSSETT, B.M. and E.C. HANSON (1975) *Interest and Ideology: The Foreign Policy Beliefs of American Businessmen.* San Francisco: Freeman.

SCHATZ, H. (1970) *Der Parlamentarische Entscheidungsprozeß.* Meisenheim am Glan: Hain.

SCHLETH, U. (1971) "Once again: Does it Pay to Study Social Background in Elite Analysis?", pp. 99–118 in R. Wildenmann (ed.): *Sozialwissenschaftliches Jahrbuch für Politik,* Band 2. München: Olzog.

SCHWARZ, H.-P. (1972)"Entspannungs-Ideologie und europäische Realitäten". *Die Politische Meinung* 17:5–23.

SONNENFELDT, H. (1978) "Russia, America and Détente". *Foreign Affairs* 56:275–294.

VAN ATTA, R. and D.B. ROBERTSON (1976) "An Analysis of Soviet Foreign Economic Behavior from the Perspective of Social Field Theory", pp. 7–36 in S. Raichur and C. Liske (eds.): *The Politics of Aid, Trade, and Investment.* New York: Halsted.

WEEDE, E. (1975a) *Weltpoltik und Kriegsursachen im 20. Jahrhundert: eine quantitativ-empirische Studie.* München: Oldenbourg.

WEEDE, E. (1975b) "World Order in the Fifties and Sixties: Dependence, Deterrence, and Limited Peace". *Peace Science Society (International) Papers* 24:49–80.

WEEDE, E. (1976) "Widersprüche in der Weltordnung unserer Zeit". *Beiträge zur Konfliktforschung* 6, Heft 3: 125–140.

WEEDE, E. (1977a) "National Position in World Politics and Military Allocation Ratios in the 1950s and 1960s: Assertions, Evidence, and Problems". *Jerusalem Journal of International Relations* 2, No. 3:63–80.

WEEDE, E. (1977b) "Threats to Détente: Intuitive Hopes and Counterintuitive Realities". *European Journal of Political Research* 5, 407–432.

WEEDE, E. und D. SCHÖSSLER (1978) "Abschreckung und Entspannung: Hypothesen von westdeutschen Eliten und ihre Bewährung in der quantitativen Forschung". Beiträge zur Konfliktforschung 8, Heft 3, 59–80.

WEIZSÄCKER, C.F. von (1971) *Kriegsfolgen und Kriegsverhütung*. München: Hanser.

WILDENMANN, R. (1967) *Macht und Konsens als Problem der Innen- und Außenpolitik*. Köln: Westdeutscher Verlag.

WILDENMANN, R. (1968a) "Politische Stellung und Kontrolle des Militärs". *Kölner Zeitschrift für Soziologie und Sozialpsychologie,* Sonderheft 12, Beiträge zur Militärsoziologie: 59–88.

WILDENMANN, R. (1968b) *Eliten in der Bundesrepublik*. Mannheim: unveröffentlichter Tabellenband.

WILDENMANN, R. (1971) "Germany 1930/1970 — The Empirical Findings", pp. 13–60 in R. Wildenmann (ed.): *Sozialwissenschaftliches Jahrbuch für Politik,* Band 2. München: Olzog.

ZAPF, W. (1965) *Wandlungen der deutschen Elite: Ein Zirkulationsmodell deutscher Führungsgruppen 1919–1961*. München: Piper.

Appendix

SIPLA questionnaire and marginal distributions from 1976 survey

INSTITUT FÜR SOZIALWISSENSCHAFTEN
der Universität Mannheim
(Wirtschaftshochschule)

68 Mannheim
Schloß

Fragebogen zum Forschungsprojekt

"Sicherheitspolitische Planungsprobleme der Bundesrepublik Deutschland"

SIPLA-Studie 74/76

Leitung: Dr. Dietmar Schössler

Mitarbeit: Dr. Edo Enke

November 1975

SICHERHEITSPOLITISCHE PLANUNGSPROBLEME DER

BUNDESREPUBLIK DEUTSCHLAND

("SIPLA"-STUDIE)

Sehr geehrter Diskussionspartner!

Wir führen eine Experten-Umfrage durch, die gleichzeitig als Kommunikationsversuch gedacht ist. Der Kreis der Befragten wurde von ausgewählten Persönlichkeiten vorgeschlagen.

Der vorliegende Fragebogen ist mit Experten diskutiert und ausgearbeitet worden. Die Antworten wurden weitgehend standardisiert, d.h. auf bestimmte Formulierungen gebracht. Dieses System macht eine optimale Auswertung der Daten möglich und erleichtert gleichzeitig die Rückgabe der Ergebnisse an die Teilnehmer dieser Studie, d.h. auch an Sie persönlich.
Unmittelbares Ziel dieser Umfrage ist die Erhebung von Expertenmeinungen zur außen- und sicherheitspolitischen Lage, zu möglichen und zu gewünschten Entwicklungen in der westeuropäischen Gemeinschaft und im gesamteuropäischen Beziehungsfeld (WÜNSCHE UND PROGNOSEN).

Langfristiges Ziel dieser zunächst auf zwei Jahre angelegten Studie ist es, im Sinne der "DELPHI-Methode" eine dauerhafte Experten-Kommunikation über sicherheits- und militärpolitische Planungsprobleme anzuregen (SICHERHEITSPOLITISCHE ÖFFENTLICHKEIT). Jeder Teilnehmer erhält alle Antworten der Befragung zurück, zugleich verbunden mit der Bitte, den -erneut vorgelegten- Fragebogen nochmals zu beantworten (="DELPHI-Methode").

Die so ermittelten Einstellungen liefern dem politischen Planer wichtige Informationen und Hinweise für mögliche Spielräume und Grenzen außen- und sicherheitspolitischer Programme.

Alle Informationen behandeln wir strikt vertraulich. Die Antworten werden anonym auf Datenträger übernommen und grundsätzlich getrennt von Ihrem Namen und Ihrer Adresse gehalten. Bei einer späteren Publizierung der Daten werden lediglich die Gruppendurchschnitte verwendet, in keinem Falle also individuelle Antworten. Die Verantwortung für alle mit dieser Studie zusammenhängenden Tätigkeiten liegt ausschließlich beim Projektleiter.

Besten Dank für Ihre Mitarbeit

Dietmar Schössler — Edo Enke

Dr. Dietmar Schössler — Dr. Edo Enke

TECHNISCHE HINWEISE FÜR DIE BEANTWORTUNG DER FRAGEN

Wir bitten Sie, Ihre Antworten auf die vorformulierten Fragen möglichst exakt zu kennzeichnen. Kreuzen Sie zu diesem Zwecke nur d i e vorgegebenen Antwortmöglichkeiten oder Alternativen an, die Ihrer Auffassung am ehesten entsprechen bzw. auf Sie zutreffen. Jeder Antwortsatz hat ein dafür bestimmtes Feld, das Sie durch ein K r e u z oder "K r i n g e l" deutlich kenntlich machen sollten, wie das nachstehende Beispiel zeigt:

Diese Spalten werden nicht ausgefüllt, sie dienen der Auswertung

reines Milizsystem (totale Wehrpflicht	
reines Freiwilligensystem	
selektive Wehrpflicht (Mischsystem)	X oder O

Die Kennzeichnung X oder O bedeutete, daß Sie in diesem Falle die 'selektive Wehrpflicht' den anderen angebotenen Alternativen vorziehen.

Bei vielen Fragen werden typische z.T. kontroverse Meinungen gegenübergestellt. Sie werden gebeten, sich für eine dieser Antworten zu entscheiden, die Ihrer Auffassung am nächsten kommt. Einige Fragen sind außerdem 'offen' (.... gepunktete Linie .....) gehalten, um Ihnen zusätzliche Möglichkeiten der Meinungsäußerung zu geben.

Bei diesen offenen zusätzlichen Antwortmöglichkeiten empfiehlt es sich, statt vollständiger Sätze lieber Stichworte oder Kurzsätze anzugeben. Die Auswertung wird dadurch wesentlich erleichtert; denn diese Antworten müssen für die elektronische Datenverarbeitung besonders nachverschlüsselt werden.

Falls Sie irgendwelche Anmerkungen zu einzelnen Fragen machen wollen, benutzen Sie bitte den evtl. freien Platz unter den Antwortkategorien. Für längere Kommentare können Sie die Rückseiten beschriften. Geben Sie in diesem Falle die Nummer der Frage mit an, damit die Zugehörigkeit klar ersichtlich ist.

GRUNDEINSTELLUNGEN UND "BETROFFENHEIT

1. GESELLSCHAFTSBILD

In den folgenden Sätzen sind drei "Gesellschaftsbilder" dargestellt, die auf eine entscheidende Aussage verkürzt sind. Jedes dieser "Bilder" rafft einige wesentlich voneinander abweichende Grundpositionen zusammen. Für welche dieser Formulierungen können Sie sich noch am ehesten entscheiden? Kreuzen Sie bitte nur e i n e Position an.

Aussage	Anzahl	Code	Spalte
In der Bundesrepublik gibt es eine große Zahl von Organisationen, Gruppen und Institutionen, die sich im großen und ganzen die Balance halten.	547	1	7
In der Bundesrepublik gibt es eine große Zahl von Organisationen, Gruppen und Institutionen, die sich zwar gegenseitig kontrollieren, jedoch weite Kreise der Bevölkerung von diesem "Kartell" ausschließen.	225	2	
In der Bundesrepublik gibt es eine große Zahl untereinander konkurrierender Gruppen, die ein "elitäres Machtkartell" bilden, das die Wahrnehmung neuer Interessen und Ideen wirkungsvoll verhindert.	87	3	

2. STAATSBILD

Wir legen Ihnen nun entsprechend formulierte "Staatsbilder" vor:

Aussage	Anzahl	Code	Spalte
Der Staat sollte nur in wohlbegründeten Ausnahmefällen in die gesellschaftliche Entwicklung eingreifen und nicht allzu viele Aufgaben an sich ziehen.	492	1	8
Der Staat sollte gerade im Interesse der Bevölkerungsmehrheit bei gesellschaftlichen Fehlentwicklungen immer eingreifen und sich auch nicht scheuen, immer mehr Aufgaben an sich zu ziehen.	185	2	
Der Staat sollte über der Gesellschaft und ihren Teilinteressen stehen, sich nicht als ausführendes Organ gesellschaftlicher Interessen verstehen, sondern autonom politisch handeln.	180	3	

3. ZUGANG ZU GESELLSCHAFTLICHER MACHT

Was ist Ihrer Meinung nach ausschlaggebend dafür, in eine einflußreiche Position zu gelangen? Wir haben zwei typische Aussagen hierzu gegenübergestellt:

Aussage	Anzahl	Code	Spalte
In erster Linie gelangt man durch eigene Leistung, Wissen und Durchsetzungsvermögen in solche Positionen.	534	1	9
In erster Linie verhelfen Herkunft, Beziehungen und Mitgliedschaften zu einer solchen Position	307	2	

4. **POLITISCHER EINFLUSS**

Über welche Möglichkeiten verfügen Sie, politische Entscheidungen zu beeinflussen?
Beispielsweise

Politische Partei	538	1	10
Gewerkschaft	169	1	11
Andere Berufsvereinigung	233	1	12
Industrieverbände	26	1	13
Andere Interessenverbände	131	1	14
Sonstige Vereinigungen (z.B. Rotary, akademische Verbindungen)	127	1	15
Kirchliche Organisationen	52	1	16
....			17
....			

5. **AKTIVE ÖFFENTLICHKEIT**

Gibt es Ihrer Meinung nach in der Bundesrepublik eine funktionierende Öffentlichkeit, die sich kritisch u n d sachkundig mit sicherheits- und militärpolitischen Problemen befaßt?

ja	142	1	18
gibt es nur in Ansätzen	598	2	
nein	118	3	
weiß nicht	3	9	

6. **"BETROFFENHEIT" IN SICHERHEITSPOLITISCHEN FRAGEN**

Inwieweit fühlen Sie sich selbst von sicherheitspolitischen Fragen "betroffen"?

bin beruflich damit befaßt	485	1	19
bin ehrenamtlich/nebenberuflich damit befaßt	180	2	
fühle mich davon betroffen (obgleich weder haupt-noch nebenberuflich damit befaßt)	186	3	
fühle mich nicht davon betroffen	11	4	

7. **GRÜNDE FÜR "BETROFFENHEIT"**

Welche der folgenden sicherheitspolitischen Probleme würden Sie besonders beunruhigen?
(Bitte nicht mehr als drei Nennungen.)

bündnispolitische Krisen der NATO	717	1	2Ø
Diskussion über Abschaffung der Wehrpflicht	127	1	21
steigende äußere Bedrohung	664	1	22
teure Rüstungsprojekte	123	1	23
Verstöße gegen die Innere Führung in der Bundeswehr	166	1	24
kritische Situationen durch abrüstungs- und entspannungspolitische Konferenzen	232	1	25
Krieg in außereuropäischen Ländern	273	1	26
			27

8. **INFORMATIONSINTERESSE**

Gibt es spezielle sicherheitspolitische Themen, über die Sie gerne mehr wissen würden?
Beispielsweise über
(Bitte nicht mehr als drei Nennungen.)

politische und militärische Strategie	433	1	28
militärische Technologie (Rüstungstechnik)	162	1	29
Gliederung, Ausrüstung, Ausbildung von Streitkräften	80	1	3Ø
Innere Führung der Bundeswehr	83	1	31
Innere Führung in anderen Streitkräfte-Organisationen	111	1	32
Wehr- und Militärpolitik der Bundesrepublik	199	1	33
Planungsprobleme der Sicherheitspolitik	324	1	34
Wehr- und Militärpolitik des Warschauer Paktes	435	1	35
Wehr- und Militärpolitik der NATO	253	1	36
Sonstiges:			37

9. **WANDEL DES SICHERHEITSPOLITISCHEN INTERESSES**

Ist in den letzten Jahren Ihr Interesse an sicherheitspolitischen Fragen und Problemen gestiegen, ist es gleichgeblieben oder hat es sich verringert?

ist gestiegen	425	1	38
ist gleichgeblieben	423	2	
ist geringer geworden	15	3	

10. **INFORMATIONSPOLITIK BUNDESREGIERUNG**

Wie beurteilen Sie die offizielle Informationspolitik der Bundesregierung bei sicherheitspolitischen Themen? Wie fühlen Sie sich durch die Regierung informiert?

ausreichend	371	1	39
nicht ausreichend	488	2	

KAØ1

11. **INFORMATION DURCH ANDERE MEDIEN**

Abgesehen von der offiziellen Regierungsinformation - woher erhalten Sie Ihre sicherheitspolitischen Informationen?

Beispielsweise:

eigener Apparat ("hausinterne Information")	307	1	40
Presse	718	1	41
Fernsehen	592	1	42
Rundfunk	377	1	43
Fachblätter, wie z.B.			
Außenpolitik	90	1	44
Wehrkunde	377	1	45
Soldat und Technik	318	1	46
Sicherheitspolitik heute	66	1	47
Beiträge Konfliktforschung	89	1	48
Europa-Archiv	166	1	49
loyal	214	1	50
Wehrforschung	81	1	51
andere Fachblätter:	187	1	52
Gesellschaft für Wehrkunde	159	1	53
Reservistenverband	151	1	54
Deutsch-Atlantische Gesellschaft	59	1	55
Sicherheitspolitische Hochschulgruppen	16	1	56
Sicherheitspolitische Arbeitskreise der Parteien	307	1	57
Gespräche mit Experten /Kollegen	476	1	58
Forschungsinstitute (und deren Publikationen)			
International Institute for Strategic Studies (IISS)	186	1	59
Stockholmer Institut für Friedensforschung (SIPRI)	85	1	6Ø
Institut für Friedensforschung und Sicherheitspolitik, Hamburg	43	1	61
Forschungsinstitut der Deutschen Gesellschaft für Auswärtige Politik, Bonn	63	1	62
Hessische Stiftung Friedens- und Konfliktforschung (HSFK)	59	1	63
Arbeitskreis Friedens- und Konfliktforschung (AFK), Frankfurt	39	1	64
Stiftung Wissenschaft und Politik, Ebenhausen	77	1	65
Forschungsinstitut für Sicherheit und internationale Fragen (FSF), München	11	1	66
Sozialwissenschaftliches Institut der Bundeswehr, München	62	1	67
Bundesakademie für Wehrverwaltung und Wehrtechnik, Mannheim	29	1	68
Industrie-Anlagen-Betriebsgesellschaft (IABG), Ottobrunn	66	1	69
Führungsakademie der Bundeswehr, Hamburg	82	1	7Ø
Sozialwissenschaftl. Forschungsinstitut der Konrad-Adenauer-Stiftung, Alfter	21	1	71
Forschungsinstitut der Friedrich-Ebert-Stiftung, Bonn	69	1	72
Friedrich-Naumann-Stiftung, Gummersbach	46	1	73
Bundesgeschäftsstelle (resp. deren wissenschaftlicher Stab):			
der CDU	110	1	74
der SPD	179	1	75
der CSU	66	1	76
der FDP	71	1	77
Sonstiges Informationsmittel:			78
....			

12. Bitte nennen Sie hier nur dasjenige Informationsmittel, durch das Sie sich in erster Linie informieren auf diesem Sektor:

.... 79/8Ø

~~KAØ2~~ 7/8 9/1Ø

AUSSEN- UND SICHERHEITSPOLITISCHE GRUNDEINSTELLUNGEN

13. **OST-WEST-VERHÄLTNIS**

Worauf beruht Ihrer Meinung nach die gegenwärtige Situation eines Nicht-Krieges zwischen Ost und West in erster Linie?

(Bitte nur eine Möglichkeit ankreuzen)

auf wechselseitigen wirtschaftlichen Interessen	115	1	11
auf dem militärischen Abschreckungssystem	607	1	12
auf gemeinsamen Interessen der Supermächte gegenüber Dritten	79	1	13
auf der entspannten Atmosphäre seit dem Ende des Kalten Krieges	56	1	14
			15

14. **WANDEL OST-WEST-VERHÄLTNIS**

In welche Richtung entwickeln sich diese Beziehungen: Mehr in Richtung Kooperation oder mehr in Richtung Konflikt?

mehr in Richtung Kooperation	291	1	16
gleichbleibend	320	2	
mehr in Richtung Konflikt	243	3	

15. **LAGE MITTELEUROPA**

Wie sehen Sie die Lage in Mitteleuropa? Ist hier der "Nicht-Krieg" stabil? Für wie stabil halten Sie den derzeitigen Zustand im mitteleuropäischen Bereich?

sehr stabil	60	1	17
stabil	573	2	
labil	214	3	
sehr labil	12	4	

16. **WESTEUROPÄISCHE ENTWICKLUNG**

Welchen Integrationsgrad der Nationen Westeuropas wünschen Sie sich?

(Bitte kreuzen Sie auf dem Schema jeweils die von Ihnen gewünschte Kombination an.)

Politikfeld	Grad der gewünschten Verflechtung			
	voll integriert	kooperierend	national-autonom	
Wirtschaft und Finanzen	476	356	18	18
Gesellschafts-u. Sozialpolitik	306	437	106	19
Außen- u. Sicherheitspolitik	700	144	12	2Ø
	1	2	3	

17. Und welchen Integrationsgrad erwarten Sie in den 80er Jahren?

(Bitte wieder entsprechendes Feld ankreuzen)

Politikfeld	Grad der erwarteten Verflechtung			
	voll integriert	kooperierend	national-autonom	
Wirtschaft und Finanzen	156	604	91	21
Gesellschafts- u. Sozialpolitik	62	448	337	22
Außen- u. Sicherheitspolitik	193	579	81	23
	1	2	3	

18. **WESTEUROPA/USA**

Welches Verhältnis sollte zwischen Westeuropa und den USA bestehen?

(Bitte entsprechend ankreuzen)

Politikfeld	Grad der gewünschten Zusammenarbeit				
	eng und kontinuierlich	eng nur in Krisenzeiten	nur lose Zus.arbeit	so wenig wie möglich	
Wirtschaftspolitik	592	131	122	8	24
Außenpolitik	634	148	62	6	25
Verteidigungspolitik	760	64	19	14	26
	1	2	3	4	

19. Und welches Verhältnis erwarten Sie in den 80er Jahren?

(Bitte entsprechend ankreuzen)

Politikfeld	Grad der erwarteten Zusammenarbeit				
	eng und kontinuierlich	eng nur in Krisenzeiten	nur lose Zus.arbeit	so wenig wie möglich	
Wirtschaftspolitik	237	264	291	13	27
Außenpolitik	272	381	149	2	28
Verteidigungspolitik	516	254	36	5	29
	1	2	3	4	

20. ROLLE BUNDESREPUBLIK

Welche Rolle sollte die Bundesrepublik künftig aufgrund ihres wirtschaftlichen und militärischen Potentials übernehmen?

		weiter zu Frage		
sollte stärkere außenpolitische Verantwortung übernehmen	312	→ 21	1	3Ø
sollte das Ausmaß ihrer internationalen Verpflichtungen beibehalten	507	→ 23	2	
sollte ihre außenpolitischen Aktivitäten eher etwas zurückschrauben	31	→ 22	3	

21. Falls: stärkere ....

Worin sollte diese stärkere Verantwortung bestehen? Beispielsweise

Position in Westeuropa verstärken			
militärisch	88	1	31
politisch	297	1	32
im UNO-Rahmen mitwirken			
an allen Aufgaben der Friedenssicherung, ausgenommen militärische Aktionen	185	1	33
an allen Aufgaben der Friedenssicherung einschließlich militärischer Aktionen (UN-Friedenstruppe)	119	1	34
in der Ost-Politik	135	1	35
in der Entwicklungspolitik	151	1	36
Sonstiges:			37

22. Falls: Aktivitäten zurückschrauben ....

Wo sollte die Aktivität etwas zurückgenommen werden? Beispielsweise

in der westeuropäischen Politik			
militärisch	13	1	38
politisch	15	1	39
in der Ost-Politik	43	1	4Ø
in der Entwicklungspolitik	29	1	41
in der Beteiligung an UN-Aktivitäten	24	1	42
Sonstiges:			43

23. **MILITÄRISCHE BEDROHUNG**

Hat die militärische Bedrohung der Bundesrepublik durch die Warschauer Vertragsorganisation (WVO) in den 70er Jahren Ihrer persönlichen Meinung nach abgenommen, ist sie gleichbleiben oder ist sie größer geworden?

Antwort	Anzahl	Code	Spalte
hat abgenommen	74	1	44
ist gleichgeblieben	308	2	
hat sich verstärkt	471	3	

24. Wie wird sich die militärische Bedrohung in den 80er Jahren entwickeln?

Antwort	Anzahl	Code	Spalte
wird abnehmen	79	1	45
wird gleichbleiben	298	2	
wird zunehmen	467	3	

25. Welcher Behauptung könnten Sie noch am ehesten zustimmen

Behauptung	Anzahl	Code	Spalte
Die wirtschaftliche Verflechtung von Ost und West erhöht die militärische Sicherheit der Bundesrepublik durch politische Entspannung.	161	1	46
Die wirtschaftliche Verflechtung von Ost und West fördert die politische Entspannung, das militärische Risiko bleibt jedoch gleich groß.	591	1	47
Die wirtschaftliche Verflechtung von Ost und West schafft zusätzliche Konfliktpotentiale, das militärische Risiko nimmt also zu.	104	1	48

26. Hat sich Ihrer Meinung nach das militär-strategische Konzept der 'Abschreckung' bewährt?

Antwort	Anzahl	Code	Spalte
Abschreckung ist friedenserhaltend	152	1	49
Abschreckung verringert die Kriegsgefahr besser als andere Maßnahmen	287	2	
Abschreckung verringert lediglich die Kriegsgefahr	356	3	
Abschreckung ist weder friedenserhaltend noch kriegstreibend	37	4	
Abschreckung ist eher kriegstreibend	19	5	

27. Wie stehen Sie zu folgenden Hypothesen?

A Die kleinen und mittleren europäischen Länder tragen zur Sicherheit in Europa bei, wenn sie die Führungsrolle der jeweiligen Supermacht akzeptieren.

Antwort	Anzahl	Code	Spalte
stimme zu	487	1	5Ø
stimme nicht zu	287	2	

B Die Sicherheit in Europa erhöht sich, wenn die kleinen und mittleren europäischen Länder außenpolitisch selbständiger handeln können.

Antwort	Anzahl	Code	Spalte
stimme zu	275	1	51
stimme nicht zu	465	2	

28. KRIEGSURSACHEN

Welche Interessengegensätze sind Ihrer Meinung nach besonders eng mit Kriegsgefahr verbunden?
(Bitte höchstens zwei Nennungen.)

Gegensätze der Sicherheitsinteressen, weil jeder Staat oder Block versucht, Sicherheit durch Überlegenheit zu verwirklichen.	304	1	52
Gegensätze der Sicherheitsinteressen, die erst durch das Wettrüsten erzeugt werden.	148	1	53
Gegensätze der territorialen Interessen, weil manche Gebiete von zwei oder mehreren Staaten beansprucht werden.	180	1	54
Gegensätze der wirtschaftlichen Interessen, die sich etwa aus der Konkurrenz um Rohstoffe und Märkte ergeben.	342	1	55
Ideologisch begründete Interessengegensätze, die sich aus unterschiedlichen politischen oder religiösen Glaubenssystemen ergeben.	594	1	56

29. RÜSTUNGSURSACHEN

Die Erklärung von Rüstungsprozessen könnte man auf zwei knappe Formeln reduzieren:

A Es wird gerüstet, weil man sich bedroht fühlt. (="außengeleitete Rüstung")

B Es wird gerüstet, weil Industrien und/oder Bürokratien daran interessiert sind. (="innengeleitete Rüstung")

(Bitte entsprechendes Feld ankreuzen.)

	1	2	3	4	
	82	Außenleitung 472	251 Innenleitung	18	
für die USA trifft zu:	nur A	vorwiegend A	vorwiegend B	nur B	57
für die UdSSR trifft zu:	nur A	vorwiegend A	vorwiegend B	nur B	58
	119	295	302	87	

30. KSZE

Sollte die Konferenz zur Sicherheit und Zusammenarbeit in Europa zu einer Dauereinrichtung werden, also eine regionale Institution zur multilateralen Regelung von europäischen Sicherheitsproblemen?

ja	502	1	59
nein	346	2	

31. KSZE - KONTROVERSE

Zwei kontroverse Argumente für und wider eine solche Dauereinrichtung lauten zusammengefaßt:

A Dagegen: Eine solche Dauereinrichtung würde auf eine organisierte Einmischung der Sowjetunion in westeuropäische Politik hinauslaufen.

B Dafür: Eine solche Dauereinrichtung würde eine langfristig für Gesamteuropa interessante Plattform multilateraler Sicherheitskooperation darstellen.

stimme eher A zu	359	1	60
stimme eher B zu	484	2	

32. **MBFR/VERHANDLUNGSSPIELRÄUME**

Bitte nennen Sie zu den (simulierten) Reduzierungsangeboten des Ostens jeweils die von Ihnen für angemessen erachtete westliche Reaktion.

Die Angebote des Ostens beziehen sich auf die Gebiete der CSSR, der DDR und Polens.

Die Angebote des Westens beziehen sich auf die Gebiete der Benelux-Länder und der Bundesrepublik Deutschland.

OSTEN bietet:	WESTEN bietet daraufhin:			
1. Sofortverringerung der Kampftruppen um 20.000 Mann	1. mehr	35	1	61
	2. gleiches	205	2	
	3. weniger	555	3	
2. Sofortverringerung aller Kampfverbände um fünf Prozent	1. mehr	31	1	62
	2. gleiches	346	2	
	3. weniger	419	3	
3. Sofortabzug eines Drittels der in der DDR, in Polen und der CSSR stationierten sowjetischen Kampfdivisionen.	1. mehr	41	1	63
	2. gleiches	238	2	
	3. weniger	540	3	

33. **MBFR/ÖFFENTLICHKEIT OST**

Könnte eine einseitige Vorleistung des Westens bei den MBFR-Verhandlungen in den östlichen Gesellschaften Reaktionen hervorrufen, die deren Führungen dann zu ähnlichen Maßnahmen - also eigenen Truppenverringerungen - veranlassen?

		weiter zu Frage		
kann ich mir vorstellen	66	→ 34	1	64
kann ich mir nicht vorstellen	789	→ 35	2	

34. Falls: vorstellbar....

Um welche innergesellschaftlichen Gruppen oder Nationen könnte es sich da handeln?

....

....

....

....

POLITISCH-ADMINISTRATIVES SYSTEM

35. PLANUNGSPOTENTIAL DER EXEKUTIVE

Über die zunehmenden Planungskapazität der Exekutive seit der Rezession von 1966/67 sind die Meinungen geteilt. Einige kontroverse Argumente hierzu lauten:

A Die Exekutive muß verstärkt planen, weil sie sonst nur noch reaktiv auf den wachsenden gesellschaftlichen Problemdruck antworten kann und somit Spielball der Ereignisse wird.

B Die Exekutive sollte keine zusätzlichen Planungsaufgaben übernehmen, weil sich schon jetzt zeigt, daß staatlich-bürokratische Planung nicht wirkungsvoll genug ist.

C Die Exekutive sollte weniger planen, weil sich schon jetzt zeigt, daß ihre Aktivität manche Krisen erst erzeugt.

stimme eher A zu	429	1	65
stimme eher B zu	344	2	
stimme eher C zu	72	3	

36. VERTEIDIGUNGSETAT

Mit welchen Maßnahmen könnte man das gegenwärtige Abschreckungspotential der Bundeswehr erhalten?

Beispielsweise:
(Mehrfachnennungen möglich)

finanzielle Maßnahmen			
Erhöhen des Verteidigungsetats	408	1	66
Konstanthalten des Verteidigungsetats	384	2	
Verringern des Verteidigungsetats	29	3	
wehr-strukturelle Maßnahmen			
Änderung des Wehrsystems			
stärkere Miliz-Komponente	134	1	67
Ausbau des Reserve-Systems	418	1	68
stärkere Freiwilligen-Komponente	300	1	69
Änderung der Streitkräfte-Organisation			
Teil-Kaderung von Einheiten/Verbänden	252	1	7Ø
Wegfall von Kommando-Ebenen	191	1	71
Änderung der Wehrverfassung			
privates Management ('beliehene Unternehmer') für zivil-ähnliche Teile der Streitkräfte	60	1	72
privates Management für zivil-ähnliche Teile der Bundeswehrverwaltung und Rüstungsorganisation	219	1	73
Übertragen hoheitlicher Teilbefugnisse auf freiwillige Vereinigungen (z.B. Reservistenverband) für nicht-etatisierbare Aufgaben der Streitkräfte	156	1	74

Sonstiges: 75

....

....

37. VERTEIDIGUNGSETAT/"KRITISCHE SCHWELLE"

Welches Ausmaß einer Etatveränderung würde Ihnen vertretbar erscheinen? Gemeint ist eine Nettoveränderung, d.h. eine inflationsbereinigte relative Veränderung gegenüber dem Gesamtbudget.

(Bitte auf der Skala den von Ihnen für vertretbar gehaltenen Wert ankreuzen.)

%	-30	-25	-20	-15	-10	-5	0	+5	+10	+15	+20	+25	+30	%
	8	2	8	4	36	53	168	284	166	45	22	7	5	35 / 21

76/77/78

38. WEHRPFLICHT UND WEHRGERECHTIGKEIT

Die Bundeswehr benötigt zur personellen Bedarfsdeckung nur einen Teil des jährlichen Aufkommens an Wehrpflichtigen. Welche Wehrstruktur würden Sie ausschließlich unter dem Gesichtspunkt der "Wehrgerechtigkeit" bevorzugen?

reines Milizsystem (totale Wehrpflicht)	286	1	79
Mischsystem (selektive Wehrpflicht)	378	2	
reines Freiwilligensystem	188	3	

39. Und welches Wehrsystem halten Sie unter sicherheitspolitischen Gesichtspunkten für sinnvoll?

Milizsystem	198	1	80
Mischsystem	563	2	
Freiwilligensystem	93	3	

KA03

40. Sollten die jeweils Nichtdienenden ebenfalls belastet werden?

ja	702	1	7
nein	143	2	

ggf. durch was?

....

....

....

41. Wie sollte künftig die Grundwehrdienstdauer aussehen? Ist die gegenwärtige Dienstzeit ausreichend?

ist zu lang, sollte lediglich 12 Monate dauern	80		8/9
ist gerade richtig (15 Monate)	409	1	10
ist zu kurz, sollte 18 Monate dauern	258		11/12

42. Was halten Sie von einer "Euro-Wehrpflicht", d.h. jeder Wehrpflichtige sollte selbst wählen dürfen, bei welchem europäischen Verbündeten er seinen Wehrdienst ableistet?

sollte eingeführt werden	250	1	13
sollte nicht eingeführt werden	599	2	

43. **WEHRDIENSTVERWEIGERUNG**

Nach den Plänen der Bundesregierung soll das bislang übliche Prüfverfahren für Wehrdienstverweigerer abgeschafft werden. Stattdessen sollen die Gemusterten wählen können zwischen Wehr- und Ersatzdienst.
Hierzu lassen sich in der Öffentlichkeit häufig folgende kontroversen Argumente vernehmen:

A Der Wegfall des Prüfverfahrens wird eine derartige Zunahme der Verweigerer zu Folge haben, daß die Einsatzfähigkeit der Bundeswehr nicht mehr gewährleistet werden kann.

B Der Wegfall des Prüfverfahrens wird keine erhebliche Steigerung der Verweigererzahlen zur Folge haben, weil ja ein entsprechender Ersatzdienst abzuleisten ist.

stimme eher A zu	244	1	14
stimme eher B zu	599	2	

44. **ALLGEMEINE DIENSTPFLICHT**

Sollte im Sinne einer Gleichbehandlung vor dem Grundgesetz eine allgemeine Dienstpflicht eingeführt werden, d.h. eine Ausdehnung der Dienstpflicht auch auf die weiblichen Staatsbürger?

ja	445	1	15
nein	411	2	

45. **BUNDESWEHR UND GESELLSCHAFT**

"Integration der Bundeswehr in die Gesellschaft bedeutet die Übernahme aller jener gesamtgesellschaftlich garantierten Wertvorstellungen und Verhaltensweisen, die mit den Aufgaben der Streitkräfte vereinbar sind". (Weißbuch der Bundesregierung 1973/74)

Wie ist hier Ihre Meinung? Ist die Bundeswehr in die Gesellschaft der Bundesrepublik Deutschland integriert, hat sie mithin (nach obiger Definition) weitgehend Werte und Verhaltensweisen aus der Gesellschaft übernommen?

Bundeswehr ist integriert	737	1	16
Bundeswehr ist nicht integriert	114	2	

46. Gibt es Ihrer Meinung nach gesellschaftliche Wertvorstellungen, die in militärischen Organisationen noch realisiert werden sollten? Beispielsweise:

Organisation der Berufssoldaten in Soldatengewerkschaften	124	1	17
Organisation der Wehrpflichtigen in Wehrpflichtigengewerkschaften	77	1	18
Teilnahme an öffentlichen politischen Demonstrationen (in Uniform)	39	1	19
Bildung von Mitbestimmungsgremien in Truppenteilen	208	1	2Ø

Sonstiges 21

....

....

....

47. **FEINDBILD DER BUNDESWEHR**

Die Bundesregierung hat im Weißbuch 1973/74 festgestellt:

"Der Wille zur Selbstbehauptung.... benötigt kein Feindbild. Verteidigungsbereitschaft ist gegeben, wenn dem politischen Gesamtsystem mehrheitlich zugestimmt wird." Wie sehen Sie diese Entscheidung? Stimmen Sie dieser Argumentation zu?

stimme voll und ganz zu	354	1	22
stimme bedingt zu	330	2	
lehne bedingt ab	107	3	
lehne voll und ganz ab	68	4	

48. **INNERER ZUSAMMENHALT STREITKRÄFTE**

Hat diese Regelung ("Kein Feindbild") Ihrer Meinung nach Konsequenzen für den inneren Zusammenhalt der Bundeswehr?

hat positive Konsequenzen	229	1	23
hat keine Konsequenzen	381	2	
hat negative Konsequenzen	234	3	

49. **KONTROLLPROBLEME NATIONALER SICHERHEITSPOLITIK**

RÜSTUNGSEXPORT

Zur Zeit wird eine Lockerung der Rüstungsexportbestimmungen von Regierung und Opposition diskutiert. Damit soll erreicht werden, daß die Rüstungsindustrie der Bundesrepublik auch an nicht der NATO angehörende Länder liefern darf. Wie ist hier Ihre Meinung?

Rüstungsexport sollte liberalisiert werden	504	1	24
Rüstungsexport sollte nicht liberalisiert werden	350	2	

49A. Falls eines der folgenden Argumente Ihrer Auffassung entspricht, kreuzen Sie es bitte an:

Der Rüstungsexport sollte liberalisiert werden, weil dadurch Arbeitsplätze gesichert werden.	364	1	25
Der Rüstungsexport sollte nicht liberalisiert werden, weil dadurch die Industrie von ausländischen Auftraggebern abhängig wird.	144	2	

Andere Argumente: ....

....

50. Was halten Sie von folgendem Argument?

"Man sollte prinzipiell aus moralischen Gründen auf deutschen Rüstungsexport verzichten - und dies ohne Rücksicht auf etwaige ökonomische Konsequenzen, die ohnedies nicht eindeutig bestimmbar sind."

stimme voll und ganz zu	137	1	26
stimme bedingt zu	159	2	
lehne bedingt ab	277	3	
lehne voll und ganz ab	277	4	

51. KONTROLLE DER RÜSTUNGSPOLITIK IN WESTEUROPA

Die Rüstungsanstrengungen der westeuropäischen Länder sind immer noch zu wenig koordiniert; die eingesetzten finanziellen Mittel werden nicht kostengünstig umgesetzt. Mit einer forschreitenden rüstungspolitischen Integration entstehen jedoch auch Kontrollprobleme. Wie stehen Sie zu folgender häufig geäußerter Meinung?

"Die Chance einer demokratischen Kontrolle der militär- und rüstungspolitischen Planung nimmt ab bei zunehmender internationaler, z. B. westeuropäischer, Integration dieser Planungen."

stimme voll und ganz zu	94	1	27
stimme bedingt zu	306	2	
lehne bedingt ab	283	3	
lehne voll und ganz ab	173	4	

52. KONTROLLE DER RÜSTUNGSPOLITIK IN DER BUNDESREPUBLIK

Wird die Bundeswehr und ihre Rüstungsplanung durch die zuständigen politischen Instanzen wirkungsvoll kontrolliert?

ja	678	1	28
nein	170	2	

SCENARIO-KONSTRUKTION: Zukünftige Entwicklung Europas

Erläuterungen zu einem Experiment:

Zum Schluß möchten wir Sie noch bitten, an einem 'Experiment' teilzunehmen.
Über die Zukunft Europas kann man verschiedene Vorstellungen haben, sowohl was wünschenswerte Entwicklungen betrifft, als auch solche, die nach dem gegenwärtigen Stand der Tatsachen zu erwarten sind.
Sie finden auf den nächsten Seiten zwei sogenannte S C E N A R I O S , worin Sie Ihre Wünsche und Erwartungen artikulieren könne.

In Schema I sollten Sie in der entsprechenden Felderkombination den jeweils von Ihnen gewünschten Zustand ankreuzen (WUNSCHSITUATION für die 80er Jahre) -ggf. auch entgegen Ihren realistischen Erwartungen.

Im Schema II geben Sie bitte dann jeweils die Stelle an, die Ihre Erwartungen am ehesten kennzeichnet, obwohl sie Ihren persönlichen Wünschen vielleicht nicht entsprechen (Prognose für die 80er Jahre).

SCHEMA I : G E W Ü N S C H T E SCENARIOS

Beziehungen	diplomatische	wirtschaftliche	militärische
USA/ UdSSR	29 Rüstungskontroll-vereinbarungen ☐ erfolgreich 752 ☐ stagnierend 78 ☐ rückläufig 18 (Wettrüsten)	30 wirtschaftlicher Austausch ☐ wächst 722 ☐ stagniert 107 ☐ schrumpft 17	31 Konfliktbereit-schaft ☐ nimmt ab 708 ☐ bleibt konstant 120 ☐ wächst 18
NATO/ WVO	32 Vertrauen auf Gewaltverzicht ☐ steigt 615 ☐ bleibt konstant 188 ☐ sinkt 34		33 Konfliktbereit-schaft ☐ nimmt ab 663 ☐ bleibt konstant 156 ☐ wächst 17
EG/ RGW	34 Institutionalisierte Kooperation ☐ zunehmend 677 ☐ stagnierend 118 ☐ rückläufig 14 (Konflikte)	35 wirtschaftlicher Austausch ☐ wächst 717 ☐ konstant 80 ☐ schrumpft 14	
EG/ USA		36 wirtschaftlicher Austausch ☐ wächst 690 ☐ konstant 132 ☐ schrumpft 20	
NATO/ USA			37 USA-Präsenz ☐ wächst 144 ☐ konstant 536 ☐ schrumpft 140
EG, intern	38 Politische Integration ☐ zunehmend 779 ☐ stagnierend 56 ☐ rückläufig 10	39 Ök. Integration ☐ zunehmend 787 ☐ stagnierend 46 ☐ rückläufig 11	
NATO, intern			40 Milit. Integration ☐ zunehmend 710 ☐ stagnierend 96 ☐ rückläufig 30
RGW, intern	41 Politische Integration ☐ zunehmend 246 ☐ stagnierend 270 ☐ rückläufig 270	42 Ök. Integration ☐ zunehmend 305 ☐ stagnierend 281 ☐ rückläufig 200	
WVO, intern			43 Milit. Integration ☐ zunehmend 146 ☐ stagnierend 314 ☐ rückläufig 350

SCHEMA II : E R W A R T E T E SCENARIOS

Beziehungen	diplomatische	wirtschaftliche	militärische
USA/ UdSSR	44 Rüstungskontroll- vereinbarungen ☐ erfolgreich 113 ☐ stagnierend 551 ☐ rückläufig 182 (Wettrüsten)	45 **wirtschaftlicher** Austausch ☐ wächst 462 ☐ stagniert 347 ☐ schrumpft 35	46 Konfliktbereit- schaft ☐ nimmt ab 121 ☐ bleibt konstant 572 ☐ wächst 150
NATO/ WVO	47 Vertrauen auf Gewaltverzicht ☐ steigt 95 ☐ bleibt konstant 527 ☐ sinkt 212		48 Konfliktbereit- schaft ☐ nimmt ab 120 ☐ bleibt konstant 569 ☐ wächst 143
EG/ RGW	49 Institutionalisierte Kooperation ☐ zunehmend 269 ☐ stagnierend 468 ☐ rückläufig 70 (Konflikte)	50 **wirtschaftlicher** Austausch ☐ wächst 535 ☐ konstant 228 ☐ schrumpft 46	
EG/ USA		51 **wirtschaftlicher** Austausch ☐ wächst 492 ☐ konstant 310 ☐ schrumpft 42	
NATO/ USA			52 USA-Präsenz ☐ wächst 80 ☐ konstant 408 ☐ schrumpft 332
EG, intern	53 Politische Integration ☐ zunehmend 326 ☐ stagnierend 455 ☐ rückläufig 58	54 Ök. Integration ☐ zunehmend 491 ☐ stagnierend 310 ☐ rückläufig 39	
NATO, intern			55 Milit. Integration ☐ zunehmend 231 ☐ stagnierend 460 ☐ rückläufig 137
RGW, intern	56 Politische Integration ☐ zunehmend 323 ☐ stagnierend 419 ☐ rückläufig 53	57 Ök. Integration ☐ zunehmend 416 ☐ stagnierend 334 ☐ **rückläufig** 43	
WVO, intern			58 Milit. Integration ☐ zunehmend 479 ☐ stagnierend 315 ☐ rückläufig 20

ANGABEN ZUR STATISTIK

Wir dürfen Sie daran erinnern, daß alle - damit auch Ihre persönlichen - Daten streng vertraulich behandelt und anonym gespeichert werden. Ihre Angaben dienen einer Gesamtauswertung, deren Qualität von der Exaktheit der eingegangenen Antworten abhängig ist. Bitte füllen Sie deshalb auch diese statistischen Fragen möglichst präzise aus. Sie selbst können dann gehaltvollere Informationen zurückbekommen. Auch wenn Sie nicht an der Delphi-Kommunikation teilnehmen, d.h. aus bestimmten Gründen Ihre Anschrift nicht mit zurückschicken wollen, sind Ihre statistischen Angaben für die Studie wichtig.

1. Geburtsjahr 19 .... — 59/60

2. SCHULISCHE AUSBILDUNG UND ABSCHLUSS

	Anzahl	Code	Spalte
Volksschule, Hauptschule	74	1	61
Mittelschule, Realschule			
einfacher Abgang	23	2	
Mittlere Reife	66	3	
Oberschule, Gymnasium, sonstige höhere Lehranstalten (z.B. Wirtschaftsoberschule, musisches Gymnasium, technische Oberschule)			
einfacher Abgang	18	4	
Mittlere Reife	66	5	
Abitur	603	6	

3. BERUFSAUSBILDUNG

	Anzahl	Code	Spalte
abgeschlossene Lehre	252	1	62
Berufsfach- und Fachschule mit Abschluß	99	1	63
Fachhochschule, Höhere Fachschule mit Abschluß (z.B. für Ingenieure, für das Sozialwesen etc.)	74	1	64
Verwaltungsausbildung für den gehobenen Dienst	62	1	65
Universität/Hochschule			
einige Semester	125	1	66
Diplom	97	2	
Staatsexamen	104	3	
Promotion	125	4	
Habilitation	17	5	

andere Ausbildung: .... — 67

4. AUSBILDUNGSSCHWERPUNKT

Naturwissenschaft und Technik	220	1	68
Wirtschaft, Handel, Finanzen	115	2	
Rechtswesen, Verwaltung	193	3	
andere Bereiche:	250	4	

5. MILITÄRISCHER STATUS

aktiv	215	1	69
Reserve	213	2	
a. D.	165	3	
kein militärischer Status	247	4	

6. MILITÄRISCHER DIENSTGRAD

keiner	204	1	70
Mannschaft	24	2	
Unteroffizier o. P.	30	3	
Unteroffizier m. P.	53	4	
Fachoffizier	16	5	
Offizier	181	6	
Stabsoffizier	197	7	
Generalstabsoffizier	76	8	
General/Admiral	22	9	

7. FALLS AKTIVER SOLDAT

Zugehörigkeit zu

Heer	135	1	71
Luftwaffe	78	2	
Marine	75	3	
Sanitätswesen	4	4	

8. FUNKTIONSBEREICH

In welchem Bereich sind Sie hauptberuflich tätig? (Bitte nur eine Nennung!)

		Code	72/73
Politik			
Bund	25	01	
Land	7	02	
Parteien			
Bundesleitung	2	03	
Stab	12	04	
Verwaltung, Ministerialbürokratie			
Bund	122	05	
Land	19	06	
anderer öffentl. Dienst	75	07	
Streitkräfte	195	08	
Industrie-Management	64	09	
Sonstige Wirtschaft	39	10	
Industrieverband	4	11	
Gewerkschaft	22	12	
Sonst. Verband	21	13	
Massenmedien (Presse, Rundfunk, Fernsehen)	58	14	
Wissenschaft/Forschung	82	15	
Sonstiges:	37	16	

9. MITGLIEDSCHAFTEN

		Code	74
Parteien:			
SPD	226	1	
CDU	111	2	
CSU	62	3	
FDP	62	4	
andere Parteien	1	5	
gehöre keiner Partei an	332	6	
Gewerkschaft	203	7	
Bundeswehrverband	202	8	
andere Mitgliedschaften:		9	

10. HEUTIGE KONFESSION

evangelisch	491	1	75
katholisch	214	2	
andere:	5	3	
keine	140	4	

11. RELIGIÖSE ERZIEHUNG

evangelisch	551	1	76
katholisch	237	2	
andere:	4	3	
keine	53	4	

12. Welche berufliche Tätigkeit üben Sie in Ihrem Hauptberuf aus? Bitte beschreiben Sie Ihre gegenwärtige berufliche Tätigkeit (ggf. mit Titel oder Dienstgrad).

----

bitte auch für:

Ehegatte: ---

Vater: ---

Mutter: ---

Hiermit bitte ich um Übersendung der Ergebnisse dieser Umfrage, die ich streng vertraulich behandeln werde, und sage meine Teilnahme an der zweiten Befragung (DELPHI-METHODE) zu.

Meine Anschrift (evtl. auch Dienstadresse):

Name, Vorname ....

....
PLZ Ort

....
Straße/Platz

Register